From Constraints to Freedom: Unleash Your Potential with the S.O.L.V.E Method

Allison A Johnson

Published by Allison A Johnson, 2024.

While every precaution has been taken in the preparation of this book, the publisher assumes no responsibility for errors or omissions, or for damages resulting from the use of the information contained herein.

FROM CONSTRAINTS TO FREEDOM: UNLEASH YOUR POTENTIAL WITH THE S.O.L.V.E METHOD

First edition. February 4, 2024.

ISBN: 979-8224626656

Written by Allison A Johnson.

From Constraints to Freedom

Unleash Your Potential

with the

S.O.L.V.E method

Written by:

Allison A Johnson

Copyright Statement: The content supplied above is the author's intellectual property and is protected by copyright laws. This content may not be reproduced, distributed, or used without the author's explicit consent.

Disclaimer

Disclaimer: This information is designed to provide competent, reliable information regarding the subject matter covered. The resources provided in this book is for general information purposes only and does not represent professional advice. The author makes no express or implied guarantees or assurances as to the information's completeness, accuracy, reliability, or usefulness. Any action done by the reader in reliance on the information provided is solely at their own risk. The author is not accountable for any errors or omissions in this information, or for any losses, injuries, or damages resulting from its use.

Preface

The principal aim of this book is to serve as a reference for individuals seeking self-discovery and advice to overcome any negative tendencies that may impede their progress.

As an author who is enthusiastic about sustainable development, I aim to support SDG 3, which focuses on promoting good health and well-being. I believe it is important to understand how negative habits are formed as it can aid in self-discovery. By acknowledging the patterns and triggers that lead to such habits, we can identify the root cause and work towards breaking the cycle. The research conducted by Palmer (2020) served as the primary reference for me as an author to explore the formation of habits and to develop an approach for cultivating new ones.

We live in a world that is beautifully designed for all to enjoy, but we face challenging situations that require resilience. This book will provide resources to help you develop the ability to bounce back and recover from difficult experiences. Additionally, the book entails resources to help you develop the power of breaking negative patterns Why? This is important to the process of alleviating the emotions of guilt or shame and cultivating a more optimistic outlook on well-being. The result is to emancipate yourself from barriers that limit your potential.

—

Introduction

This book provides inspiration as you create a roadmap for realizing the significance of this life-changing experience and the ability of beneficial habits to create a purposeful existence. First, acknowledging that some habits are inherited from parents allows an individual to recognize that certain behaviors or patterns that they exhibit may not be your responsibility. It may enable you as the reader to be more empathetic and nonjudgmental to yourself when attempting to modify your behaviour.

Second, evaluating inherited habits has a strong potential to provide new perspectives on the underlying causes of habit creation and change. Researchers in article American Psychological Association (2020) were able to identify patterns and elements that contributed to healthy behavior.

I was then able to apply the concepts to this guide to subsequently develop strategies for eliminating negative habits by studying how patterns are passed down through generations. This research was further helpful in developing the techniques mentioned in this book as a framework for breaking undesirable inherited habits and establishing favorable ones. More importantly, exploring inherited behaviors is important to self-discovery, as it is an important part of the process allowing individuals to obtain better knowledge of their behavior and motivations.

Self-reflection can lead to increased self-awareness and insight into one's values, objectives, and ambitions. The exploration of the impact of negative inherited habits from parents was beneficial in this process. This was especially important for developing the concept of modifying behavioral patterns and contributing to self-discovery through the S.O.L.V.E method.

Some of the resources in this book are additionally supported by an article by the American Psychological Association (2011). The reference was made to develop this book as self-discovery is critical in the process of learning how to break undesirable behaviors from generational traits. First, when a person takes decisive action, they intentionally decide to face their challenges directly. This proactive approach enables them to analyze the situation, explore potential solutions, and make sound decisions.

You will learn critical thinking skills by assessing options, weighing consequences, and taking effective actions during this process. Additionally, you will start taking decisive action and improve your confidence to make a positive impact. You will gain confidence in your problem-solving ability and cultivate a sense of self-efficacy by actively addressing your difficulties. This confidence in your abilities helps create a positive self-image and confidence to help you overcome existing and potential challenges.

Chapter 1

Chapter 1: Understanding Negative Patterns

Cultivating A Mindset to Embrace Change

As you embark on the first chapter of this transformative journey, you are taking your first intentional step towards battling the negativities that lurk in the shadows of your life. This marks the beginning of a deliberate approach towards personal growth and development to battle those negativities that lurk in the shadows of your life. These negatives may have somehow impacted your life and possibly prevented you from achieving your maximum potential.

You may agree that some of these negative factors include communication barriers and self-doubt. These factors can limit your potential due to fear of success and anxieties. The strategies in this book provide an invitation to recognize and accept change in your life based on a specific strategy. Throughout the stages of life, you sometimes find yourself at a turning point, where you may be faced with decisions that are difficult to make.

This book is a valuable resource that provides motivating ideas and words of encouragement to help you ignite your motivated spirit and dissociate from negative generational patterns. Think for a moment about the patterns that you want to break. *Is it an inherited fear of taking chances from your ancestors? Or maybe an inclination for self-harming behaviours passed down is like an unseen inheritance?* Discovering these patterns is one of the critical steps on your path to freedom. If you're feeling anxious about showing off your unique gifts because of parental expectations, don't worry...you're not alone. The situation may be difficult to confront, particularly when you feel like you are suffocating your creativity. You are at another intersection, where you can take a closer look at where priorities lie and discover the foundation in which they were constructed. It's important to separate inherited goals from your genuine impulses.

As you start the process of self-discovery, you may need to peel back some layers to uncover your hidden essence. This is because external influences often create expectations that can obscure your true nature. This process can be scary, but it's a necessary step to move forward. The scope of moral choices might be concealed by uncertainty and fear at times but necessary for your growth. In this step, you can start to identify the difficulties you encountered, while dealing with uncomfortable situations that demanded you to speak up for your moral values.

It acknowledges the psychological struggle...the uncertainty, doubt and fear that often cloud your ethical decisions. The S.O.L.V.E method can serve as your trusted companion in fostering your moral courage. The method will guide you in navigating through difficult situations and empower you to take transformative actions. It's about identifying the anxieties that have subtly influenced your choices, comprehending how they show up in your life, and realizing how they affect your overall well-being. I urge you to respond to this assessment candidly. Regard this as an introspective dialogue with yourself in which exposure becomes the first step toward comprehension. Take a moment to reflect on this: *What choices have my genetic tendencies influenced? How have they quietly crept into the matrix of my well-being?* The purpose of this reflection is about exploring the complexities of your inner landscape, rather than passing judgment. The goal is to lessen the impact of concerns, not to eliminate them. Let's now examine the strategic attitude shift that underpins our goal.

If you decrease the level of an intense history this might make the framework of your true self stronger. This tactical strategy entails actively confronting inherited tensions, casting doubt on their credibility, and progressively reducing their impact on the way you think. Think of each worry as an invader in your mental sanctuary. Play the part of a vigilant guard; when they linger longer than necessary, confront them, investigate their motives, and deliberately lessen their influence rather than giving them the building's keys.

This is an extended effort that is gradually developing, demonstrating your dedication to creating a life free from the constraints of inherited recurring phobias. Let us now delve deeper into the world of mindfulness, an exceptionally effective associate on your journey to emancipation. The path to rescue yourself from the entanglement of inherited negative generational cycles, is a gradual process that requires intentional effort. Envision every action as a deliberate decision to free yourself. This is your chance to unlock the door and discover the enormous expanse of your unrealized possibilities. Imagine yourself on this path to transformation; feeling lighter with each step, releasing the responsibilities of generations past, and relishing the freedom to write your script to your amazing story. *Recognizing the negative patterns that need to changed*. You may sometimes view life as a puzzle, with each piece reflecting a distinct feature. Within each puzzle piece are generational cycles and challenges inherited from the previous generations. These concerns, though often subtle, act as influential forces shaping our mental terrain, guiding our viewpoints, and steering our decisions.

Recognizing and breaking free from these unseen bonds, is a challenge. It requires not only self-awareness, but also an organized approach for significant transformation. Your inherited concerns build the foundation of your thinking in a manner that goes unnoticed a great deal of the time. They penetrate the very core of your mind, influencing your thoughts on life, relationships, success, and even failure. The task is yours to recognize the presence of these problems and comprehending their subtle yet persistent impact on your daily life. Subsequently, these decisions manifest as anxieties, biases, or limiting beliefs that guide your decisions.

Here is an example: A genetic fear of insecurity may lead a person to pursue a more conservative job route, even if their passion lies elsewhere. The influence is significant, shaping the course of our lives in ways we may not fully comprehend. Breaking the rules beyond generational concerns takes more than just acknowledgement; it demands a well-planned approach. The S.O.L.V.E method works as a road map; pointing individuals to a deliberate process of self-discovery, monitoring, and eventually, emancipation. In this transformative journey, you will delve into the complexities of your specific issues, which are linked to inherited negative patterns and generational cycles. You will venture into the depths of your self-discovery challenges, revealing regions that are ideal for empowerment. Set your mind free from the bonds of limiting ideas and infuse your path with transforming power specific to your aspirations. You are disrupting the patterns that held you back by using personalized resilience measurements to progressively break the grip of inherited fears. As you nurture positive patterns necessary for your transforming journey, you may be faced with a common challenge: the weight of parental judgments. I want you to envision yourself standing beneath the weight of parental expectations in the ethos of personal transformation narratives.

We are now taking a more in-depth look at the transforming impact of the S.O.L.V.E method. You will discover that it is more than just a phrase; it is the key to crafting a new story. During your life, you may have faced this typical challenge: overcoming hurdles while adhering to generational customs. In this continuous journey, it is recommended to utilize the transformative S.O.L.V.E method, to guide you. Your issue right now is not only about overcoming obstacles, but also about changing your patterns of handling similar issues that may arise.

You are learning how to develop generational limitations and see your victory materialize. You are still in the early stages of your journey and each challenge that you overcome, represents a step closer to becoming a competent version of yourself. You may experience a feeling of limitation because of communication barriers that may stem from generational communication patterns. *Can you envision yourself at a defining moment, restricted by impediments to communication, and intertwined in the rules of communication across generations?* A prevalent issue that you may face involves being confined by generational cycles that obstruct personal milestones. You can be free from being trapped in the clutches of generational cycles which restrained you from achieving your personal milestone. You are now able to escape constricting concepts using S.O.L.V.E as an aid to overcome barriers as you set and achieve personal goals. It is an inevitable victory once you apply the transformative S.O.L.V.E method in the process. *Are you able to visualize yourself breaking free from the constraints that inhibit your individual growth by the bonds of generational cycles?*

You have the power to evade limiting concepts; S.O.L.V.E is your tool to overcome barriers as you set and achieve personal goals. Your inherent patterns of worries might be like a relentless habit, tearing at the infrastructure of your ambitions. These problems frequently span generations and perhaps resulted in a whirlpool of feelings relating to anxiety. *Are you ready to identify these patterns, comprehend their origins, and consciously manage generational currents?* The navigating tool of S.O.L.V.E , will be that tool that you apply to eliminate those worries.

You have the power to cultivate the empowering spirit of your path. Allow yourself to be free of constraining notions.... those self-imposed limitations and be open to the endless possibilities that this shift brings. You have the S.O.L.V.E toolkit and the innate power to start reducing the barriers to your personal development. Remember that you are not alone while you manage the currents of inherited concerns. We all carry remnants of the past with us. The steps to this journey are small, yet filled with potential because you are armed with the S.O.L.V.E attitude. You have the toolkit to guide you to develop the power of evicting thoughts that have constrained you. You have the unrestricted potential to embrace your journey and break out of the concepts that constrain you. You're not only on a path to emancipation, but you are also creating your successful story.

Typical domains for individual growth

Financial Empowerment: Limiting beliefs can put an overarching cloud over your financial path, making it critical to tackle any obstacles that may hinder your sense of economic empowerment. You will learn to navigate by employing the S.O.L.V.E technique. With this revolutionary strategy, you will develop the skill of learning to disconnect from the web of limiting beliefs. The strategy is designed to enable you to make deliberate decisions that lead to your financial well-being. Financial empowerment is the result of deliberate choices. By actively utilizing this strategy, you have a chance to shape your financial future.

Make decisions that align with your goals, values, and aspirations. It's a steady path towards financial independence, one deliberate action at a time. Measure how you're doing financially as you continue the expedition. The S.O.L.V.E method not only helps to dissolve the bonds of limiting ideas, but it also functions as a metric for growth. Track the intentional choices you make and witness the tangible results.... a step closer to financial empowerment. Financial empowerment is the result of your deliberate choices. You are now on a conscious pathway to shape your values and ambitions. It's the route toward financial independence, one deliberate decision at a time.

Emotional Intelligence: This can often be overshadowed by generational patterns which may sometimes be undetected because of social or cultural tendencies. As you progress in your transformational journey, you start to become more emotionally aware. You will break free from the shackles of a lack of emotional intelligence; guided by the transformational power of the S.O.L.V.E approach. If you incorporate this in your daily life, then you will develop the skill of managing the complexities of your emotions. It is an immersive experience of self-awareness and empathy, aided by deliberate emotional learning.

Each deliberate step you adopt, will assist you in unravelling the components, empowering you to embrace a deeper knowledge of emotions. You will learn how to effectively leverage the transformative power of the S.O.L.V.E approach and separate your focus from emotional unintelligence. When you intentionally incorporate this in everyday activities; you will help people understand the intricate details of emotions. Additionally, you will develop empathy and self-awareness. Be vigilant as it relates to the increased complexities of emotional intelligence and a reduction in the influence of generational emotional tendencies. The S.O.L.V.E method helps to eliminate the bonds that bind your emotional intelligence, facilitating the way for authenticity and a deeper connection with your emotional self.

Restricted Mindset: As you continue your transformative journey, you're now exploring the path to wisdom. You have learned from the insights gained through dedication to the strategic processes and continue to develop in meaningful ways. One of the junctures you may face in personal development is where you are confronted by the daunting impediment of a *restricted mindset*. This may have been influenced by cultural conditioning; this refers to the system of beliefs that shapes your values, attitudes and behaviours. We have all been on this path. You perhaps have wrestled with the constraints of your perceptions. You are on a consistent path of developing a forward-thinking mindset. *How do you pivot when life throws you curveballs?* It is not only about solving problems; it is also about the mindset you bring to the table.

The S.O.L.V.E strategy will be your helpful tool in assisting you to keep track of your reactions to problems within this realm. Be ready to accept change, embrace uncertainty and let these trials shape you into the person you're meant to be. *Are you ready to rework the script and shift from that restrictive viewpoint?* You have the solution to infuse motivation with the dynamic S.O.L.V.E technique, and watch as your personal development becomes not just a goal, but a way of life. You will now be able to achieve your full potential.

Lack of Self Compassion: As you continue this trajectory...you may have many instances where you pause and self-reflect on various aspects relating to self-discovery. Another issue you may have struggled with is the lack of self-compassion. This may have been influenced by your social upbringing; you may have struggled with the issue of practicing self-compassion amid parental projections. Your cultural conditioning may have created a cloud over your mental capacity to treat yourself with care and empathy. In this journey, you may have started to accept imperfections as being a regular part of the human experience. This would have allowed you to welcome moments of self-kindness by starting to nurture self-compassion.

Regard this as a beckoning to break free from the bonds of self-criticism and embrace self-compassion. Self-compassion is essential for inner calm and resilience. It is a beautiful journey towards a more compassionate relationship with yourself. You cultivate self-compassion when you actively take steps to nurture your mental and emotional well-being. This may be nurtured by prioritizing your own needs and engaging in self-help methods. The experience of cultivating self-compassion is extremely important because it represents a conscious choice to break free from the chains of self-criticism.

Acknowledge the effects of your parental expectations and use the S.O.L.V.E method as a guide in the process of developing self-compassion. You are able to leverage this method and make it an everyday habit to cultivate compassion and to see the beauty in imperfections. Evaluate your development using the S.O.L.V.E approach and enjoy the significant moments of self-compassion victories. You will witness the constraints of the lack of self-compassion start to diminish, as you start to blossom into a more empathetic version of yourself.

Building Inner Confidence: As your path to personal development unfolds, you may think about ways to build your inner confidence. Your perspective on gaining or showcasing confidence may be connected to patterns inherited from your parental or cultural expectations. You are encouraged to place significant focus on handling difficulties relating to confidence. You will utilize introspection to identify those that are especially impacted by cultural norms. Cultural standards may have casted a shadow over your path to self-assurance; this now urges you to face your issues head-on. The S.O.L.V.E method is an innovative strategy that can help you achieve your objective of cultivating inner confidence. It is a means of empowerment designed strategically to aid you in breaking free from negative conventional standards and cultivate a strong sense of self-assurance. This is focused on helping you to tenaciously assemble the courage to welcome this life-changing experience. You will ultimately be empowered to rise above the limitations of these expectations.

You will then be able to assert an entirely new level of self-assurance that is in complete harmony with yourself. Take control of this life-changing journey, by seizing this exceptional chance to write this new chapter. You will be more empowered to progress towards a life that is in line with your genuine goals and embrace a more confident and honest version of yourself. Developing inner confidence is a process, not an instant gain...it is a continuous process as new opportunities may arise in which you need to exert confidence. You are encouraged to foster moments of self-assurance utilizing the S.O.L.V.E method as your guide. Additionally, you will gain insight into the distinctive attributes that influence your personality. It is a journey towards a more honest relationship with yourself. As the days progress, keep an eye out for moments of self-assurance.

Career Choices: As an individual, you may have felt restricted by your personal choices in choosing a career. This is your chance to identify fundamental passions and talents, thereby revealing the genuine professional self that may have been veiled by familial expectations. *Can you identify any situations in which these expectations have influenced your professional decisions?* You have the opportunity to critically examine your family's expectations in influencing your career choices; determine whether they correspond with your objectives or serve as chains binding you to unfulfilling pathways. In the process of self-reflection, you will start to cultivate a mindset that will help you to contemplate your professional choice as a chance for growth. *Are you caught in a maze of professional stagnation, where the weight of limiting ideas and familial expectations have influenced your choices?*

You are encouraged to perform a thorough self-examination to uncover the foundations of limiting ideas that operate as concealed roadblocks to professional advancement. You may find yourself within the complex structure of familial expectations, acknowledging that, while well-intended, they may have inadvertently hindered professional growth. Challenge these expectations assertively, recovering control over your career path. Embrace the difficulty of challenging cultural conventions, determining which components are authentic and which are relics of obsolete beliefs.

The great news is that you can construct a fresh perspective for your career path; one that is completely in line with your values and goals. This will require a detailed action plan that breaks down large goals into achievable steps. Measure your progress utilizing the S.O.L.V.E method. You will note the occasions where you can cultivate professional growth and adjust your career path if this is within you goal. Seek mentorship and assistance in addition to using the S.O.L.V.E method and use collective wisdom to move your career ahead.

Aligning Personal Goals: It's a process of nurturing intention in every activity and ensuring that it correlates with your values. The primary problem is a disconnect between sincerely held principles and the decisions made in your daily life. If you are at the point where you need to establish alignment; it is necessary to be intentional about your values. This is critical because it is a conscious step towards adopting integrity, ensuring that every action reflects the foundation of your core values. *How are you feeling so far on your journey to transformation? Did you know that your personal goals must be aligned with daily behaviors to live an authentic life?*

Recognize that you are currently reviewing the discrepancies between your values and your activities. In this trajectory of self-reflection, acknowledge the internal conflict that develops when your choices do not align with your underlying beliefs. This path may also challenge you to face your mistakes head-on. This transformative strategy acts as a signal that steers you in the direction and reconciliation of principles and conduct. You will learn to negotiate the risks of daily decisions, ensuring that they are consistent with your strongly held notions. In order to align your values and behaviour this requires a continuous effort hence; you are propelled to examine your values frequently. This is possibly through self-reflection in the progress of affirming your principles and reassessing your decisions with the S.O.L.V.E method as your strategic guide. You have the solution.....The transformative S.O.L.V.E method...an effective bridge-building tool that encourages you to constantly examine your values and make conscious decisions that reflect your fundamental principles.

You must actively reassess your values frequently, to make deliberate choices that align with your underlying principles. It is a constant journey to integrate your goals into all aspects of your personal life. The S.O.L.V.E approach is now your blueprint, bringing you to the complex terrain of options and helping to ensure that each decision reflects the credibility of your principles. You continue to measure instances of consistency as you grow. You will be cultivating a profound feeling of integrity in every action.

Establishing Personal Boundaries: Personal boundaries are the components of your ability to cultivate autonomy and self-respect. You will agree that establishing personal limits is a critical step on the path to self-discovery and empowerment. It is more than just a necessity; you are mentally establishing a statement of self-esteem and a commitment to personal development. You need to establish boundaries to foster genuine connections and protect yourself from the negative effects of overcommitment. You will be in a better position to establish a space where you can thrive and be free of other people's criteria. Establishing personal boundaries can be a challenging process, especially if you are not socialized in a culture that emphasizes the importance of doing so. This will be a purposeful step towards cultivating satisfying relationships, in which each personal connection represents a healthy blend of mutual respect and individual autonomy.

The main issue at hand is to establish clear boundaries. You will start exploring the specifics of setting limits in relationships, particularly when familial expectations are involved. This stage of your trajectory is another unique opportunity to utilize the S.O.L.V.E method in your tactic to consistently set and maintain healthy boundaries. You will learn to communicate more effectively, convey your wants, and establish relationships. You will be able to document situations where individual autonomy is exercised, and boundaries are successfully established and upheld. The successful application of the S.O.L.V.E method along with your willpower will guide you in creating and maintaining healthy boundaries while providing you with a sense of empowerment in personal relationships. The ability to purposefully establish boundaries will allow you to live to a life that is intentional and meaningful.

Leadership Development: Your mission continues, and the emphasis is now geared toward personal leadership development empowering you to lead. This is where you will gain insight into how to combat the limiting ideas that may be hampering your development as a leader. If you lack confidence, you can learn to establish this through the transforming S.O.L.V.E technique. It is advisable to seek mentorship to track your leadership development and successes. The process will enable you to recognize and overcome those limiting ideas that may be preventing you from reaching your full leadership potential. Subsequently, these impediments now become opportunities for growth and transformation rather than roadblocks.

In this journey, you are advised to seek mentorship. One of the most important advantages of mentorship, is that you benefit from the wisdom and direction of experienced leaders. The impact of this can be measured by the improvements to your personal leadership growth and accomplishments with the guidance of the S.O.L.V.E method. The use of metrics is extremely important as you will be required to track the milestones whether tangible or intangible. The intangible aspects consider things such as improved confidence, polished skills, and a stronger sense of purpose. Take a moment to reflect on why this is important to you.

You could reflect on this to be an upward move in the trajectory of your personal development. This will guide you towards being a more confident and effective leader. This is essential because your leadership development propagates into your professional and personal realms. The results of this will have a beneficial impact on the people you lead or may lead. Once you can achieve this goal: it will have far-reaching implications. The goal is to become a more confident and effective leader and inspire people around you. This will have an excellent rippling effect in both your family life, business, and personal domains.

Exploring Personal Passions: You have taken yet another progressive step in your journey. The emphasis is now on exploring your passion.... those things that excite you, bring out your inner passion, interest, etc. As an individual, you may sometimes feel disconnected from personal passions owing to family/ societal expectations. This may be due to expectations based on the impact of parental expectations or the weight of responsibilities. This may have prevented you from achieving your passions. An example could be...you have always wanted to own a bike, but your social conditioning as a child conveyed that bike riding would result in the likelihood of an accident.

Pursuing personal interests is a key technique for improving mental health. It relieves stress, gives a sense of accomplishment, and contributes to overall emotional resilience. If you can make a deliberate attempt and devote time to your interests; you will achieve a better balance. The goal to drive you to prioritize your mental health by embracing those passions that makes you happy. The S.O.L.V.E technique helps you set limits and make deliberate choices that prioritize your interests, ensuring a harmonic balance between family, professional and personal interests. You will discover that passion fuels creativity and innovation, hence immersing yourself in what you enjoy.

Subsequently, this allows you to tap into your creative reservoir, unleashing fresh ideas and insights which may benefit numerous aspects of your life, including family, work, and relationships. When you engage in activities that you are passionate about, this will result in a more beneficial impact in your relationships. This process promotes and invites you to share your passions with others, develop deeper connections and mutual understanding.

Nurturing Your Moral Choices: The scope of moral choices might be concealed by uncertainty and fear at times. In this step, you will begin to recognize the challenges that you may have faced. You may be confronted with unpleasant situations that require speaking up for moral beliefs. It acknowledges the psychological struggle...the uncertainty, doubt, and fear that often cloud ethical decisions. This is where the S.O.L.V.E method emerges as your guide in the framework of cultivation of unleashing your moral courage. This revolutionary approach is supportive, as you navigate the difficulties of ethical judgment. It is advisable to continue to apply the S.O.L.V.E method to break down the walls of fear and uncertainty, allowing your inner moral courage to surge.

Moral courage's heartbeat is assertive; therefore, you are urged to practice assertiveness, a skill that enables you to communicate your beliefs with assurance and clarity. This is where the S.O.L.V.E method comes into play, breaking down all the obstacles that may be hampering your ability to stand up for what is morally right. Moral courage is a practice, not a one-off deed and is an expression of your dedication to these principles. Fostering moral bravery is an example of integrity in a world where ethical standards might be questioned. Each act of moral courage becomes a milestone in your journey, a witness of your dedication to your goals.

Balancing Social Activities and Establishing Personal Space: The perpetual pursuit continues as you learn how to balance social activities and enjoy your personal space. This is important to your overall well-being. The approach inspires a desire for self-improvement by addressing the obstacles brought by social demands. Achieving balance allows you to negotiate social obligations gracefully, while maintaining the sacredness of your personal space. You will be able to nurture a sense of accomplishment and contentment. As individuals a frequently encountered difficulty is feeling overwhelmed by society's expectations and the need for regular social connection. Recognize these feelings without personal bias and remember that balance is essential. You can cultivate fundamental strength with the help of the S.O.L.V.E technique in navigating the complexities of establishing healthy boundaries while offering practical solutions.

This may guide you to a place of acknowledging your need for personal time, whilst maintaining good social relationships. The strategy for unlocking potential is to achieve a balance between social interactions and personal space, this fosters deliberate choices and intelligent time management. This routine allows you to establish an approach that works for you, subsequently allowing you to enjoy social interactions. Additionally, you will enjoy the rejuvenation that personal space brings. You will be required to benchmark your success in psychological well-being because of a balanced approach to achieve it with the help of the S.O.L.V.E method. Visualize the benefits of intentionally establishing boundaries that boosts your energy levels, mental clarity, and emotional resilience.

This is where you discover the rhythm that resonates with your unique essence...this lies at the heart of personal harmonization. The S.O.L.V.E method allows you to be more in tune with your inner needs. The responsibility is yours in ensuring that your social interactions are sources of joy and connection rather than draining obligations. This will involve creating a routine that works for you boost your energy levels and promotes general well-being. Importantly, cultivating harmony doesn't mean abandoning personal space. The S.O.L.V.E strategy helps you strike a balance in which social connections improve your life balance while preserving your vitality.

Personal space is your regeneration sanctuary, an essential component of long-term well-being. The balance between your social time and personal space should be more than simply a logistical consideration. It is a significant investment in your mental and emotional wellness. The S.O.L.V.E approach method helps you to cultivate self-mastery and enables you to set healthy boundaries. The benefits of this are not limited to ensuring an appropriate equilibrium between your social interactions and valued personal space.

Cultivating Healthy Habits: Get ready to start cultivating healthy habits as we continue your transitioning journey. The main priority is helping you to overcome unhealthy habits may affect your overall well-being. *What is the solution?* cultivate wellness with the effective S.O.L.V.E technique. Cultivating healthy habits should not be just simply a short-term objective; instead, it should be a long-term endeavour to cultivate a lifestyle that coincides with your well-being goals. This will aid with your adoption of modest lifestyle adjustments that will create the way for a healthier and happier existence. The moment that you tackle the unhealthy habits that have taken root and negatively affecting your overall health, you are taking an active step. This is accomplished by actively recognizing the patterns that retard your well-being. In the process, you need to recognize and understand that change is not only possible but also mandatory for your regenerative path.

It is advisable that you implement moderate lifestyle changes rather than advocating for radical changes. It will be easier for you to accommodate moderate lifestyle adjustments. The S.O.L.V.E method enables you to discover specific areas for improvement and assists you in making conscious decisions that contribute to your overall wellness. Keep track of your general well-being, recognizing the good impact of the changes you've made. Do not neglect to keep track of the adoption of healthy patterns that will assist you in navigating toward a better lifestyle as you move forward. Your primary concern should encapsulate actively designing a routine that, aligns with your well-being goals and fosters a vibrant sense of health-conscious decisions.

This will serve as the foundation for the future transforming chapters of your life. Bear in mind that cultivating a healthy lifestyle should be more than simply a short-term objective; it is a long-term endeavour to cultivate a lifestyle that coincides with your well-being goals. This is the connection that unites your journey of developing a way of life that is in line with your well-being goals. You are encouraged to intentionally design a lifestyle that supports your ideals and fosters a vibrant sense of self. This forms the foundation for your future transforming chapters, resulting in a journey of continuous progress and fulfilment.

How will I be able to achieve this? The impact of your personal development journey extends beyond independent objectives and penetrates every aspect of your life, ultimately affecting your general state of well-being. Imagine the profound impact on your mental health as you overcome unfavourable negative generational habits that you have inherited. A feeling of empowerment takes the place of diminished anxiety. You grow emotionally stronger and can handle life's adversities with grace. Your authenticity fosters deeper connections as you learn how to develop meaningful relationships. Think about how your goals affect your entire faculties with happiness and fulfilment in addition to your accomplishments. Align your growth path with the profound realization that harmony across your life, rather than strictly achievement in one area. This is a necessary component of meaningful prosperity.

During your life, you may face this typical challenge: overcoming hurdles while adhering to generational customs. In this continuous journey, it is recommended to utilize the transformative S.O.L.V.E method, the recommended technique for this part of your journey. You may be at a turning point, attempting to tackle obstacles in life while complying with deeply rooted generational standards. Ultimately, the S.O.L.V.E method will be instrumental in helping you to overcome inclinations and eliminating phobias carried over from earlier generations. It is important to remember you still have to utilize tangible metrics to measure the success in these stages. This is mandatory for tracking the steps designed to help you overcome those hurdles. It is time to reclaim the charge of your identity by constructing a tale that connects with your genuine self and encourages the development of self-awareness.

Rewriting your personal story is growth which is essential in the field of personal development. Maintain that journal and note the intimate details of your development. Capture occasions when you become more self-aware and when you reject cultural demands to be authentic to yourself. This is not just about rewriting your story; it is also about celebrating your accomplishments along the way to reality. Therefore, on this important date, start to rewrite your story. Take hold of your identity and embrace the power of the S.O.L.V.E method. You will have the opportunity to let your record of events become an affirmation of the achievements of self-awareness and authenticity. Your progress will be more than just another page in the construction of your strong, true self.

Cultivating Spiritual Connection, The insatiable search for personal greatness continues, and you are at an iconic moment: evaluating the necessity of establishing a spiritual connection. It's easy to feel disconnected from our spiritual anchors while facing life's chaos. This is a call to action to reestablish or cultivate that connection and reap numerous rewards that can be gained from spiritual fulfilment. It is essential that amid the chaos of daily life, you cultivate a spiritual connection; this is vital because this produces equilibrium.

It is an opportunity to create a sacred space for personal meditation and to hear the whispers of your soul. The results create a deeper awareness of your spiritual nature. These practices, whether tiny acts of gratitude or more extensive spiritual activities establish a pattern of connection. *Are you ready to incorporate specific actions into your daily routine?* The S.O.L.V.E method makes it easier to include these routines, transforming them into transformative acts that nurture your spirit. The genuine nature of spiritual connectedness is found in the benefits it provides.

As you engage in personal introspection and rituals guided by the S.O.L.V.E process, you will experience a greater sense of spiritual fulfilment. This is your adventure, a self-discovery composition, in which the beauty of your spiritual nature unfolds, creating a great sense of fulfilment and tranquillity. The establishment of a spiritual connection extends beyond individual fulfilment to a sense of being connected beyond oneself. You may think of this as achieving a higher purpose and feeling connected to something bigger. The most important aspect of this journey is the enhanced spiritual fulfilment that comes with a powerful sense of contentment and calm.

Balancing Independence and Collaboration: Allow yourself to go a step further and cultivate an atmosphere of emancipation by balancing independence and collaboration. Life's unpredictable events may sometimes cause difficulty in balancing personal autonomy while facilitating the desire for shared experiences. *Are you ready to make room for the game-changing methodology of S.O.L.V.E to help you take centerstage?* The S.O.L.V.E strategy is strategically designed to help in navigating you through the delicate balance of pursuing this personal goal.

Additionally, you are allowing others the opportunity to share in your personal space while establishing your own level of autonomy. This trajectory will allow you to recognize and value your individuality within a collective environment. The empowerment blueprint of S.O.L.V.E is strategically designed to help you in finding solutions. You are now using its dynamics is now being used to create a harmonious blend where individual endeavours and collaborative moments coexist smoothly.

The success measurements will help you to track increased harmony in balancing personal and shared activities. Your distinct characteristics, goals and interests are valued as crucial components that contribute to the diversity of your collective experience. The beauty is that you have the freedom to be authentic in establishing your personal space while facilitating others. You may thrive better in an environment that emphasizes both freedom and shared experiences, resulting in a holistic feeling of well-being. The advantages extend beyond the present moment, creating an atmosphere for long-term connections and personal fulfilment.

Establishing Intimate Relationships: By now it is established that you are on a path of progression. In this part of your journey, you are given particular attention to developing trust in your intimate relationships. Your focus should lie on overcoming trust concerns and creating a climate that values open communication and honesty. The current section goes beyond simple problem-solving to explore the rich rewards that emerge when trust becomes the foundation of your intimate relationships. This is an ongoing journey where personal empowerment is devoted to the development of trust in intimate relationships.

You are making a more intentional and purposeful effort to foster transparency in your intimate relationships. Transparency becomes the foundation of fostering inclusivity which is allowing you to communicate your thoughts, feelings, and vulnerabilities without fear of being judged. The benefits involve exploring the rich rewards that emerge when trust becomes the foundation of your intimate relationship. Recognize that you are on a purposeful venture to foster transparency in your intimate relationships. You are making room to overcome trust concerns and create a climate that values open communication and honesty.

By doing this you are fostering inclusion which allows for your partner to communicate their thoughts, feelings, and vulnerabilities without fear of being judged. You may appreciate that an emphasis on constant communication contributes to the relationship's overall well-being. Maintain the use of the S.O.L.V.E method to track your improvement in relational happiness while settling your individual concerns.

The continual conversation becomes a source of joy, connection, and shared progress. You are also establishing a resilient partnership that will withstands life's ups and downs. In a nutshell, developing regular communication contributes to the path to a relationship distinguished by profound emotional connection, trust, security, increased intimacy, and general well-being. This is a beautiful journey where you are discovering the gems hidden beneath the rewards. Each step is an affirmation of the transformative power of consistent and open communication while cultivating lasting love and connection.

As your level of trust matures, your mentality evolves into one of security and reassurance. As a couple, you will feel safer knowing you can count on your spouse for support, understanding, and unwavering commitment. These benefits go beyond the alleviation of trust difficulties to contribute to a healthy relationship in which both parties feel seen, heard, and cherished. The exciting new is you can break free from the unseen bonds that anchor you to defunct accepted practices. It all starts with a bold act of self-reflection and an unshakable desire to call the fundamental structure of society standards into question.

It's about asking the question that matters most: *"Is this expectation serving my growth, or is it merely a relic of the past, handed down like an heirloom without consideration for its relevance to my unique journey?"* Breaking free demands an unrelenting discovery of your individuality. It's about accepting the inconsistencies, passions, and dreams that make you uniquely you. It's a call to arms, a declaration that deviating from a conventional is not only acceptable, but phenomenal. Your path to autonomy entails fearlessly accepting the events of your life and an unwavering determination to live life on your terms.

Let us now discuss exceeding societal expectations. You are a warrior wielding the sword of critical thought, society's expectations may have once felt impassable, but empowered with the tenacity to challenge, you become an unstoppable force. You are not being rebellious you are developing foresight, you are sifting through the various layers of history and rejecting what no longer adds value to the decision-making pattern of your ambitions. Remember that your path to breaking free is not a single undertaking. It's an integrated transformation in which one's act of resistance helps to shift societal expectations.

By questioning the existing normal, you not only empower yourself but also emerge as a torch for those seeking the bravery to embark on their road of self-discovery. In a nutshell, the route of breaking free from generational cycles and cultural expectations is a celebration of your uniqueness. You will learn to nurture your inner strength, challenge the narratives that have been negatively imposed on you, and establish a path that resonates with your own passions. The world will be waiting to meet your true, emancipated self.

Chapter 2: The S.O.L.V.E Strategy

Introduction to S.O.L.V.E

Let's proceed into the S.O.L.V.E Method, a framework that empowers you to overcome the deeply entrenched patterns imprinted by your lineage, chapter by chapter. According to the article by Palmer (2020) you accumulate insights into the complexity of developing habits as time progresses. This will look into the perspective of learned associations to draw insights into how the learned patterns stemming from your parents' habits may produce lasting traces of your behaviour. This path to self-discovery delves into the unnoticed connections that exist between acquired behaviors and the way you communicate. The research primarily focused on the modification of habits; however, the concept was critically analyzed, and aspects were developed to show the impact of parental behaviors on inherited negative patterns.

(S)Specify the Challenge/Problem.

Throughout life, a person may experience restricted anxieties, fears and doubts which may surprisingly be inherited from generational cycles. In general values and anxieties are deeply rooted in many societies, passed down through generations like prized artwork. This may be developed from habits or repeated patterns as individuals may find themselves following standards and anxieties just because their ancestors did. To break free from these cultural shackles, one must actively question, challenge, and redefine deeply held beliefs.

According to research by Palmer (2020), habits arise through repeated activities in the same setting, according to the University of Southern California's Habit Lab. According to the lab's findings, a large amount of human behaviour is habitual, which means it is executed automatically without conscious decision-making or willpower. They discovered that around 43% of daily behaviours are performed routinely.

Habits are learned linkages between reactions and features of the context in which they occur, such as physical location and prior activities. The lab focuses on the function of context signals in habit formation and how habits can endure despite social effects when conducted in familiar settings. Cultural experiences that elicited fear reactions, whether of the unknown or specific threats, might be transmitted down the generations. Recognizing and overcoming these deeply rooted anxieties requires an awareness of the evolutionary background as well as consciously selecting a different route. To break free from these cultural chains, a conscious and intentional effort to question and challenge firmly held beliefs is required.

This approach necessitates self-reflection, open-mindedness, and a willingness to consider various viewpoints. Individuals must overcome the discomfort that might occur when challenging long-held customs or societal expectations. Introspection is necessary for personal growth and autonomy. Questioning existing values and worries does not always imply complete dismissal of them. On the contrary, it entails an evaluation and redefinition process based on individual experiences, ideals, and changing societal settings.

Individuals can maintain aspects of their cultural history that correspond with their personal beliefs while eliminating or changing those that restrict personal development or lead to unwarranted worry because of this careful examination. Let's be transparent for a second. *How often do you find yourself on autopilot, reacting to things in an almost pre-programmed manner?* It's as if you're running on default settings and breaking free from that cycle requires an extensive change in your decision-making approach. Intentional decisions are more than just choices; they are declarations of your autonomy as an individual. Contemplate the following: each the decision you make is an advancement in your life's journey.

Instead of allowing your feet to follow a known course of generational patterns, here is the time to choose the trajectory that resonates with your core values, ambitions, and desires. Reflect on this: *how many times have you said yes to something because your parents, grandparents, or society expected you to?* It's time to put a halt to the habitual impulses and start making decisions that reflect your genuine self.

Your intentional decisions may often result in positive outcomes if carefully strategized It's about pausing, thinking about your principles, and asking yourself, *"Does this choice align with who I am and where I want to go?"* It is the solution to the knee-jerk reactions bound into the substance of negative generational habits. Breaking free involves breaking the cycle, and deliberate decisions are your one-of-a-kind arsenal. You have the power to break the cycle of automatic solutions and instead choose with intention. This is a conscious decision about recovering your capacity to make conscious, clear, and honest decisions. Intentional decisions result in positive outcomes. You are now clearer about the process, therefore, the next time life throws you an unexpected challenge, hit the pause button, take a deep breath, and make a decision that resonates with the rhythm of your spirit.

(O): Offers Positive Solutions

Positive behaviours provide the foundation of your new story as you break away from inherited cycles. Consider these habits to be the structure of your life, influencing your ideas, behaviour and overall well-being. The daily routines that create your character and define the quality of your life are the building blocks of transformation. You may view these habits as emancipators rather than constraints. They provide a framework that encourages progress, instils discipline, and creates a good mindset. Identify habits that are in line with your goals. Let the affirmations of your dedication to a meaningful and purpose-driven existence be positive habits, healthy routines, or mindful practices. Your ultimate purpose of breaking free is to live a meaningful life.

Your unique experiences, values, and goals deserve an active role in developing your perception of the world. It's about giving yourself that chance to develop into a more harmonized version of yourself with your present situation. Let's explore more deeply how patterns can be broken. Your first step in this stage is to recognize and address the need to break patterns that are no longer beneficial to your personal development. This may entail deliberately selecting alternate behaviours, attitudes, or viewpoints that disrupt rooted generational patterns. *Are you willing to seize the bull by the horns and shake things up?*

If you're exhausted from repeating the same old song countless times and want to break free from the bonds of generational patterns that have kept you hostage, you've made the ideal step. The development of positive behaviour and emotional resilience will produce ripples that impact every coast of your well-being. Reflect on this ripple effect to be the framework that assists in modifying the structure of your life... mental, emotional, and social. As you progress, examine the influence of your changing behaviours on your mental health. *Do you feel empowered, as if you have control over your choices?*

Take note of how enhanced emotional resilience transcends emotional well-being and permeates your relationships. Intentional decisions are sometimes just rewriting the script and embracing a story that is uniquely yours, not just generating a new pattern in your life. In your daily life, attitudes may have a subtle but profound influence. Breaking negative patterns entails changing those attitudes and viewing your issues as hurdles to seeing them as chances for growth. You have complete command concerning developing an attitude that pulls you forward and remember your perspectives are the lenses through which you view the world. You are actively breaking free from inherited notions and striving to see the world through your perspective.

As you delve further into the complicated pattern of behavioural changes and emotional resilience, you start to focus on breaking free and creating a life full of positive habits using the S.O.L.V.E method. You will start to manifest along this journey, through the discoveries that you learn throughout this process; offering insights to inspire you on this journey of self-discovery and freedom for complete transformation. The impact of this transformative approach extends beyond individual interactions. This shapes the collective dialogue within your sphere of influence; you can take control of your life and unleash your full potential. This is where you continue to empower your journey and start breaking free from limiting beliefs and embracing transformative power. This is done through a series of carefully crafted strategies. You learn to offer positive solutions that focus on personal empowerment, encouraging intentional choices, and break negative patterns. One of the key components of positive solutions is personal empowerment. Personal empowerment entails recognizing one's importance in constructing one's own life, independent of generational pressures. You are not just a viewer on the infinite platform of life; you are the author, administrator, and leading star of your extraordinary success.

Let's begin on a fantastic expedition of personal empowerment; a journey that celebrates your ability to design your story and navigate from predictable patterns influenced by past generations. Your life is a dynamic, ever-evolving story with many options waiting to be explored; not a fixed plot imprinted in concrete. Personal empowerment is the realization that you control the pen, and each mark you make on the blank page of your life contributes to the exceptional work that is your life.

You can use this to regain control of your life from the grasp of generational pressures. This means tuning into your GPS and manoeuvring through your unique goals, rather than repeating a script set by others. This can be viewed as a unique role given to you; you can rewrite your own story and introduce plot twists that reflect your deepest aspirations and ideals. Personal empowerment begins with a significant realization: you are the author of your own life story. It's about recognizing the impact of generational expectations and embracing the fact that you have the freedom to diverge from the expected plotlines. Break free from the constraints of tradition and move into your own spotlight. *Do you get tired of feeling like life just happens to you? Are you ready to take control and direct yourself to the territories of intentional living?* If your answer is yes, you are ready to delve into the explosive domain of conscious decision-making, the key elixir to breaking free from the phase of autopilot that has you captured in those generational patterns of behaviour.

(L) means (Lay Out Growth Metrics)

Adopting a metrics-based approach is critical for your progress and breaking free from the confines of inherited negative behaviours. This keeps you in alignment and rather than obsessing on abstract goals, you can focus on concrete indications that represent our progress towards resilience and liberation. Tracking progress entails, a thorough analysis of your growing resilience. Simultaneously, you examine the declining impact of inherited negative behaviours, limiting beliefs, and concerns that have kept you captive for far too long.

You can then appreciate the fact that growth measurements are vital since they drive you towards change. In essence, you do not only anticipate change, but you also must quantify it. By establishing these concrete milestones, you empower yourself to celebrate each step forward, each obstacle you overcome, and every instance in which the weight of inherited burdens is lifted. Your assessment's clarity is what makes it significant. This is where you now must identify and document instances where resilience has increased. You do this by noting where harmful patterns have lessened and limiting beliefs have been replaced with empowering realities. This approach instils a sense of accomplishment, which strengthens your dedication to the transforming path.

Your measures go beyond mere observation; they form the feedback loop required for long-term growth. It is then imperative that regular reviews are done using predetermined parameters. You can agree that growth is not a single boost, instead, it follows an ongoing rising trajectory. Therefore, each step confirms your growth, recognizing small triumphs, while modifying your direction as needed. You will appreciate the fact that this metrics-driven method is not a rigid set of rules, but rather a tailored path to self-discovery and empowerment. By meticulously tracking your accomplishments and losses, you make an intangible concept of transformation a tangible reality.

This is a practical method for creating a meaningful life, making quantifiable progress toward freedom, and creating a narrative characterized by resilience and positive transformation. It is imperative in the S.O.L.V.E strategy as this step allows you to gauge progress by measuring adjustments for your success. For example, increased resilience and diminishing impact of inherited anxieties. It depends on the specific problem that is being dealt with. To overcome these underlying issues, a structured strategy encompassing tracking and measuring growth measures must be adopted.

Assess your ability to recover from setbacks. Your inherited concerns from generational cycles may limit you at times; this is a frequent difficulty that typically goes undetected. These worries become embedded in one's mentality, impacting viewpoints and influencing decision-making. Increased resilience suggests that you are making headway in overcoming the emotional burden of inherited fears to achieve your best life. To gain control over your life's trajectory, it takes an organized approach that requires dissecting the complexity of these problems, dividing them into smaller components, and thoughtfully addressing each one. The process of tracking and assessing growth is fundamental to this technique. It's like creating a visualization into the impenetrable corners of one's intellect, which shows that there are hidden worries and fears there. Individuals can employ this tracking technique to detect patterns, triggers, and repeated themes, providing vital insights into the origins and nature of inherited anxieties.

It's an in-depth evaluation of the mental environment that paves the path for strategic actions to be implemented to tackle these issues. Evaluation parameters take into consideration critically examining observed behavioural changes, taking note of situations where decisions and behaviours deviate from inherited negative patterns. You are encouraged to notice the tangible changes that serve as visible indicators of development. Examine your emotional reactions to difficult events. Increased emotional resilience means that you are getting better at distancing yourself from the emotional impact of inherited concerns.

(V) Verify Personal Progress

This step of the journey is essential to ensuring that your journey is on track, and you understand the relevance. You may envision it to be a step-by-step process that involves breaking free from inherited anxieties and generational cycles. It is critical to have a structure in place for evaluating personal progress to properly travel this road. This not only emphasizes the effectiveness of selected techniques but also performs as a motivator, reinforcing your dedication to growth. As you progress further in the step-by-step process of releasing yourself from the bonds of inherited negative generational cycles we venture farther into the domains of self-discovery and transformation.

You are now applying the S.O.L.V.E method to identify, track changes set goals to help you overcome these challenges while documenting your success. You are encouraged to maintain a journal, record the times you overcame obstacles, and notice how the impact of inherited worries is lessened. Picture the transformational force of the S.O.L.V.E method to guide the trajectory in helping you to overcome this particular challenge.

Your issue right now is not only about overcoming obstacles, but also about changing your patterns of handling similar issues that may arise. You are learning how to develop generational limitations and see your victory materialize. You are still in the early stages of your journey and each challenge that you overcome represents a step closer to becoming a competent version of yourself. Pledge your dedication to true relationships, embracing honesty, mutual understanding, and shared ideals. As you reflect on this journey, visualize creating your revolutionary communication philosophy. Commit to incorporating thoughtful decision-making into all interactions, transforming conversations into a form of expression that symbolizes your enlightenment path. Your philosophy functions as an affirmation of your commitment to meaningful connections and true self-expression.

It reflects the revolutionary attitude of breaking free from inherited communication standards, resolving the way for a life full of true interactions and meaningful interaction. It's about depth over surface-level interactions and depth over quantity. Ask yourself what the importance of true relationships on your path to emancipation is. Genuine connections provide comfort, understanding, and a sense of belonging. These connections serve as anchors, anchoring you in your pursuit of personal growth and breaking free from negative inherited habits. You will learn to appreciate the fact that building true connections calls for a plan based on honesty, mutual understanding, and shared values. By embracing mindful communication, you are utilizing the S.O.L.V.E blueprint for building the connection between each interaction. Every component symbolizes an important component that contributes to the overall framework of true connections.

(E) embracing mindful communication and nurturing authentic connections.

This section will provide you with an in-depth comprehension of guidance for mindful communication. You will learn to appreciate prioritizing the development of genuine relationships over surface-level encounters. You will start to nurture connections based on honesty, mutual understanding, and similar goals. As time progresses you will learn to incorporate deliberate decision-making into your communication approach. An important factor in the process of fostering mindful communication is to pause and reflect on the impact of your words on both you and others before replying to any conversation. It is recommended that you utilize metrics for enhanced communication. This is where you examine the validity and significance of your relationships to determine the depth of your connection.

A stronger sense of connection demonstrates fulfilment in overcoming generational communication barriers. You should assess your capacity for handling arguments with mindful communication. Successful conflict resolution demonstrates an advanced method for handling challenges, without prejudice due to generational communication habits. Honesty is what forms the basis of genuine relationships which is the firm basis upon which trust is created. Being truthful to yourself and others creates an environment in which authenticity can flourish. Communicating your thoughts, feelings, and vulnerabilities with openness allows for reciprocal honesty in your relationships. By cultivating honesty, you will unmask incredible benefits even as this measure helps you break free from generational communication patterns. You will appreciate the fact that discovering honesty propels you to express your true self. An example of honesty would be not avoiding tough conversations but embracing them even when they seem uncomfortable.

This could be analyzed as an effective framework that bridges the distance between people, generating understanding and compassion. You may discover that appreciating and understanding other points of view and experiences; produces a sense of connectedness that minimizes generational communication barriers. Mutual understanding serves as a connector between individuals. The primary advantages of mindful communication include enhanced communication quality and accuracy of information transmission. Some of the benefits of this include increased attention focus, reduced attentional biases, improved relationship level communication, higher personal growth, a sense of competence, autonomy, and relatedness etc.

Mindful communication will also lead to lower levels of negative affect and higher levels of positive effects. Additionally, this includes improved emotion regulation, composure in stressful situations, constructive conflict resolution, mutual acceptance and caring, and increased psychological safety and intimacy. Mindful communication has the potential to significantly improve human growth by cultivating these personal and interpersonal qualities. It can improve self-awareness, self-regulation, and emotional intelligence, resulting in more effective conflict resolution, beneficial relationships, empathy, and compassion Johannes [1]et al (2019).

How does this mindful communication benefit intimate relationships?

The practice of mindful communication will also benefit your intimate relationships. Johannes et al (2019) conducted research to explore the benefits of mindful communication. The study found that practicing mindful communication led to numerous advantages. The impressive benefits further include: lower levels of negative emotions, higher levels of positive emotions, better regulation of emotions, ability to remain composed in stressful situations, improved communication quality, constructive conflict resolution and a sense of mutual acceptance among couples.

You are now at an important juncture in which we will be gaining an in-depth exploration of your relationships. This is a criterion for your emancipation path. You will learn to master the art of conflict resolution which serves as a compass for navigating the intricate web of generational communication obstacles. This is able to assist you to review the legitimacy and relevance of your relationships.

I want you to further evaluate your relationships to be a means of evaluation for determining the quality and value of your connections with others. This investigation probes below the surface to examine the fulfillment received from overcoming generational challenges to communication. View your interactions

---

[1]. https://www.frontiersin.org/people/u/586425

as "surges on the outermost layers of a rough sea" Envision that beneath the waves are unknown depths that determine the genuine nature of connection. By going into these depths, you can evaluate the legitimacy of your relationships. *Do you feel deeply satisfied or do surface-level relationships leave you wanting more?*

Consider the influence on the depth of connectedness of breaking out from generational traditions of communication. *Has the journey enabled you to establish deeper ties that go beyond the constraints of planned interactions?* A stronger awareness of connection demonstrates your growth and the purposeful effort you put into cultivating true relationships. Mindful communication may be considered as the "lighthouse that guides us across the turbulent waters of conflict" or a "competent captain sailing a ship over turbulent waves" avoiding the rocks of misunderstanding and animosity.

You may evaluate your conflict resolution mastery by assessing your ability to handle conflicts with conscious communication. Successful dispute resolution demonstrates your progress and evolution. Regard your conflicts not as battles won or lost, but as opportunities for growth and relationship strengthening. Evaluate the impact on conflict resolution of breaking out from generational communication habits. *Has your path equipped you to approach issues with a proactive and understanding mindset?* Successful conflict resolution becomes evidence of your advanced methods, demonstrating the paradigm-shifting potential of mindful communication. The art of mastering conflict-solving is not an easy process therefore, the following practical strategies are designed to help you navigate using mindful communication techniques. These tools may act as your navigator guiding you through the storm and breaking you free from the cycle of generational communication habits.

Foster improved communication with these strategies

Successful Pause and Reflect: Use a pause-and-reflect method during a quarrel. Take an introspective approach, evaluate your feelings, and consider the flip side of the other party's viewpoint. This purposeful pause prohibits knee-jerk reactions established in negative generational habits. Strategies for developing resilience and coping with adversity can be linked to the concept of mindfulness communication. Mindful communication is being fully present and attentive to your relationships with others, as well as being aware of your thoughts and emotions.

This is consistent with the resilience-building methods discussed in the context, such as connecting, accepting aid and support, and engaging in good activities to alleviate stress and negative emotions. When you engage in mindful communication, you connect with others and receive help and support. This involves actively listening and being present with those who care about them.

Furthermore, finding good strategies to relieve stress and negative sentiments, as well as taking decisive measures, can be considered parts of mindful communication. You can intentionally choose how to respond to difficult events and emotions. Furthermore, as indicated in the context, cultivating a good self-image correlates with the concept of mindful communication. *How?* You nurture others by encouraging them to believe in their abilities, S.O.L.V.E problems and trust their intuition. This is likely to have a positive impact on how they communicate with others. In conclusion, the tactics discussed in the context of building resilience and coping with adversity are related to the concept of mindful communication because both emphasize the necessity of being present, self-aware, and purposeful in our interactions and answers to difficult situations.

Allow yourself to go a step further and cultivate an atmosphere of emancipation by balancing independence and collaboration. Life's unpredictable events may sometimes cause difficulty in balancing personal autonomy while facilitating the desire for shared experiences. *Are you ready to make room for the game-changing methodology of S.O.L.V.E to help you take centerstage?* The S.O.L.V.E strategy is strategically designed to help you navigate through the delicate balance of pursuing this personal goal. Additionally, you are allowing others the opportunity to share in your personal space while establishing your level of autonomy. This trajectory will allow you to recognize and value your individuality within a collective environment.

The empowerment blueprint of S.O.L.V.E is strategically designed to help you develop solutions to your problems. You are now using its dynamics to create a harmonious blend, where individual endeavours and collaborative moments coexist smoothly. The success measurements will help you to track increased harmony in balancing personal and shared activities. Your distinct characteristics, goals and interests are valued as crucial components that contribute to the diversity of your collective experience. The beauty is that you have the freedom to be authentic in establishing your personal space while facilitating others. You may thrive better in an environment that emphasizes both freedom and shared experiences, resulting in a holistic feeling of well-being. The advantages extend beyond the present moment; creating an atmosphere for long-term connections and personal fulfillment.

Chapter 3

Chapter 3: Overcoming Personal Roadblocks

Fostering Authenticity and Embracing Mindful Communications

Fostering Genuine Connections: This section will provide you with an in-depth comprehension of guidance for mindful communication. You will learn to appreciate prioritizing the development of genuine relationships over surface-level encounters. You will start to nurture connections based on honesty, mutual understanding, and similar goals. As time progresses you will learn to incorporate deliberate decision-making into your communication approach.

An important factor in the process of fostering mindful communication is to pause and reflect on the impact of your words on both you and others before replying to any conversation. Throughout this book, you have gained a deeper understanding of how informed decisions help you to break free from negative generational communication norms. This will be further highlighted in this section embracing mindful communication.

The guidance in this book will be the roadmap to developing true relationships that go beyond the surface, in line with your goal to break free. You will be able to gain a better understanding of how prioritizing honesty and intentional communication may become the foundation of your game-changing approach to interactions. An important tip for nurturing mindful communication is to prioritize genuine relationships over momentary encounters for a fulfilling life. It would be valuable to consider evolving from a full gathering of acquaintances to a cozy circle of genuine connections. The road to improved thinking can be compared to a book with chapters in which you discover new knowledge as you progress. The difference is in this case; you are the writer and the primary focus of this story. Your mindset's evolution is an exciting narrative that is waiting to be published and every realization and every strong reaction to adversity brings you to the recognition that your life is not prewritten. As you evaluate your level of resilience, acknowledge small steps towards improvement, and reframe challenging circumstances, picture the outcome of your changing perspective as being in line with your ideal of independence and empowerment.

As you continue this path to autonomy, resilience becomes an important criterion for progress. It functions as a measuring instrument, measuring the ability to recover from setbacks, face challenges and bear the emotional burden of generational concerns. In this situation, resilience is more than just a psychological trait; it is an active, measurable response to the structured method adopted American Psychological Association (2011).

Your setbacks have been reconstructed as opportunities for progress, rather than obstacles. Overcoming setbacks becomes an essential component of the emancipation process, indicating not only victory over current problems but also a profound revolution. It's a journey of self-discovery, finding hidden strengths and nurturing resilience that demonstrates personal growth. In essence, overcoming generational concerns is not an automated process. It entails a process of self-awareness, purposeful intervention, and resilience formation. The proposed structured technique serves as a guide, a tool for individuals to travel through the intricacies of their inherited problems and emerge on the other side. The path to release from your inherited generational concerns is both complex and empowering. The design entails a critical analysis of one's mental environment, a planned strategy for tracking and measuring growth and an investment in resilience as a progress indicator. By seeing setbacks as opportunities for advancement, you can reroute your course and break free from the inherited worries that have silently constituted your destiny. The planned strategy will prov to be more than a guide; it is the key to unlocking the door to life.

This will help you to be free of the constraints of the past shackles that once limited their potential. As you engage on this journey, you will discover the search of resilience for future generations. Your mission continues and the emphasis is now geared toward personal leadership development, empowering you to lead. This is where you will gain insight on how to combat the limiting ideas that may be hampering your development as a leader. The measures will help establish confidence through the transforming S.O.L.V.E technique.

It is advisable to seek mentorship to track your leadership development and successes. The process will enable you to recognize and overcome those limiting ideas that may be preventing you from reaching your full leadership potential. Subsequently, these impediments are now opportunities for growth and transformation rather than roadblocks. In this journey, you are advised to seek mentorship. One of the most important advantages of mentorship is that you benefit from the wisdom and direction of experienced leaders. The impact of this can be measured by the improvements to your personal leadership growth and accomplishments with the guidance of the S.O.L.V.E method. The use of metrics is extremely important as you will be required to track milestones whether tangible or intangible. The intangible aspects take into account things such as improved confidence, polished skills, and a stronger sense of purpose. Take a moment to reflect on why this is important to you. You could reflect on this to be an upward move in the trajectory of your personal development, guiding you toward being a more confident and effective leader. It should be essential because your leadership development propagates into your professional and personal realms; having a beneficial impact on the people you lead or may lead.

Once you can achieve this goal it will have far-reaching implications. The goal is to become a more confident and effective leader while inspiring people around you. This has an excellent rippling effect in both your family life, business and personal domains. The perpetual pursuit continues as you learn how to balance social activities and enjoy your personal space. This is important to your overall well-being. This approach inspires a desire for self-improvement by addressing the obstacles brought by social demands. You will be able to achieve balance and negotiate social obligations gracefully, while maintaining the sacredness of your personal space.

This will nurture a sense of accomplishment and contentment. As individuals, frequently encountered difficulty is feeling overwhelmed by society's expectations and the need for regular social connection. Recognize these feelings without personal bias and acknowledge that balance is essential. You can cultivate fundamental strength with the help of the S.O.L.V.E technique in navigating the complexities of establishing healthy boundaries while offering practical solutions. This may guide you to a place of acknowledging your need for personal time whilst maintaining good social relationships. The strategy for unlocking potential is to achieve a balance between social interactions and personal space, this fosters deliberate choices and intelligent time management. This routine allows you to establish an approach that works for you. You will subsequently enjoy social interactions in addition to the rejuvenation that personal space brings. You will be required to benchmark the success in your psychological well-being as a result of a balanced approach with the help of S.O.L.V.E .

Some of the benefits of intentionally establishing boundaries include: boosting energy levels, mental clarity and emotional resilience. This is where you discover the rhythm that resonates with your unique essence...this lies at the heart of personal harmonization. The S.O.L.V.E method allows you to be more in tune with your inner needs. The responsibility is yours in ensuring that your social interactions are sources of joy and connection rather than draining obligations. This will involve creating a routine that works for you to boost your energy levels and promotes general well-being. Importantly, cultivating harmony doesn't mean abandoning personal space.

The S.O.L.V.E strategy helps you strike a balance in which social connections improve your life balance while preserving your vitality. Personal space is your regeneration sanctuary, an essential component of long-term well-being. The balance between your social time and personal space should be more than simply a logistical consideration. It is a significant investment in your mental and emotional wellness. The S.O.L.V.E approach method helps you to cultivate self-mastery and enables you to set healthy boundaries. The benefits of this are not limited to ensuring an appropriate equilibrium between your social interactions and valued personal space.

Competent Communication Strategies

You are now at an important juncture in which we will be gaining an in-depth exploration of your relationships. This is a criterion for your emancipation path. You will learn to master the art of conflict resolution. It serves as a compass for navigating the intricate web of generational communication obstacles which helps review the legitimacy and relevance of your relationships. I want you to further evaluate your relationships to be a means of evaluation for determining the quality and value of your connections with others.

This investigation probes below the surface to examine the fulfillment received from overcoming generational challenges to communication. View your interactions as "surges on the outermost layers of a rough sea" Envision that beneath the waves are unknown depths that determine the genuine nature of connection. By going into these depths, you can evaluate the legitimacy of your relationships. *Do you feel deeply satisfied or do surface-level relationships leave you wanting more?* Take into account the influence on the depth of connectedness of breaking out from generational traditions of communication. *Has the journey enabled you to establish deeper ties that go beyond the constraints of planned interactions?*

A stronger awareness of connection demonstrates your growth and the purposeful effort you put into cultivating true relationships. You may evaluate conscious communication. You can master the art of developing competent communication strategies, establishing an environment where different points of view are appreciated and nurtures connections between people. You can overcome generational communication barriers, paving the opportunity for profound connections. True self-expression is essential for empowerment.

Consider it a "brilliant morning", removing the shadows of self-doubt and conformity. By honestly expressing your thoughts and feelings, you empower yourself and uncover the hidden potential within. Consider previous occasions where generational communication habits may have limited your ability to express yourself. *Did the weight of judgement or expectations obscure the light of your actual self?* Mindful conversation becomes the key to breaking free from these restraints and revealing your true self.

Mindful communication questions these habits by bringing a deliberate approach to dispute resolution. Active listening, empathy, and a dedication to discovering mutually beneficial solutions are all required. You are now at the point where you start to evaluate the transforming power of intentional interaction in conflict resolution beyond instances of disagreement. Your solution to handle disagreements with empathy and collaboration becomes an example, improving your relationships by achieving greater connection and mutual growth.

Take a moment to examine the repercussions: *How has mindful communication transformed the dynamic from conflict to collaboration? Is the resolution of arguments becoming a trigger for better ties, and overcoming the boundaries of generational communication habits?* The transforming impact extends beyond confrontations, affecting the broader landscape of your relationships. You are encouraged to adopt thoughtful communication as a tool for empowerment. Practicing mindful communication enables true self-expression wherein you can contribute toward your own and others' empowerment. Mindful communication can help you break free from generational communication patterns by honestly expressing your views and feelings. It takes an innovative, deliberate approach to fostering understanding and connection. The power of breaking free from generational communication patterns requires an innovative approach, a departure from the scripted dialogues of the past. Envision it as a journey of exploration, where each interaction becomes an opportunity to redefine the narrative. Mindful communication is the navigating principle that will help to guide you through uncharted territories of understanding and connection.

Consider the power of intentional communication in disrupting ingrained habits. *Have you found yourself using phrases or responses inherited from past generations without conscious thought?* Mindful communication requires a deliberate pause, an intentional choice to respond in a way that aligns with your authentic self. Mindful communication tactics build connections by respecting and valuing different points of view. Consider these tactics to be building blocks that allow for the open exchange of ideas and experiences. You can create an environment where varied points of view are not only acknowledged but embraced by using intentional communication.

Consider how generational communication patterns may have stunted respect for varied viewpoints. *Were certain points of view disregarded or ignored because of pre-existing norms?* The use of competent communication tactics breaks down communication barriers; allowing for deep partnerships based on mutual understanding and respect. Your conscious communication tactics build connections by respecting and valuing different points of view. Think about these tactics to be building blocks that allow for a free flow of ideas and experiences. You can establish an environment where varied points of view are not only acknowledged but embraced by using intentional communication. You are at another reflective juncture where you are encouraged to pause and assess how generational communication patterns may have stunted respect for varied viewpoints. *Were certain points of view disregarded or ignored because of pre-existing norms?*

Competent communication tactics break down these barriers, allowing for meaningful connections based on mutual understanding and respect. *Have you ever had an encounter where a well-chosen remark or a thoughtful reaction destroyed barriers that generations had built?* Generational communication barriers may pose barriers to making meaningful connections. Think of competent communication tactics to be the tools that break down these barriers, establishing the way for a seamless mission toward understanding. Each strategy symbolizes a step forward, an intentional decision to overcome the limits of the past. Take into account the role of intentional communication in bridging generational divides. These approaches form the building blocks of intentional interaction, empowering you to contribute to your growth while establishing bridges of connection with those around you.

By embracing these approaches, you will be able to communicate more effectively, listen more attentively and foster an atmosphere of mutual understanding and trust. You will learn the art of reflective listening; a technique in which you not only hear but also fully understand the speaker's point of view. Reflection is necessary in the ongoing journey to clarify your journey in fostering meaningful partnerships. By acknowledging and reaffirming the other person's viewpoint, you are intentionally building a stronger connection. You may view this from the angle of alignment of values where you identify and communicate your basic values. This is where you start to incorporate these beliefs into your speech, ensuring that your words are consistent with those values that matter. Empathy exercises are another technique in which you learn to cultivate empathy by engaging in activities that enhance your knowledge of the feelings and experiences of others.

This empathetic perspective improves your ability to respond compassionately and sincerely, allowing you to break free from generational communication habits. You are encouraged to maintain a communication log to chronicle your intentional decisions and their consequences. Reflect on the times when thoughtful decision-making resulted in more meaningful interaction. This reflective activity highlights the benefits of deviating from imposed communication patterns. Adopt expressions that empower both you and others with whom you communicate. Embrace open communication, which allows for the honest sharing of views, feelings and viewpoints without fear of judgment. Active listening is a vital component of conscious communication. Listening and fully understanding others builds an atmosphere of tolerance.

This lays the foundations for decreasing communication issues established in generational cycles. You may classify this as the key to unlocking the door to genuine connections and breaking away from generational patterns of communication. Let's investigate more thoroughly into real-world strategies that will empower you and others around you. This will simultaneously establish a safe space for honest expression and understanding. Communication is an extremely potent tool that can either limit or empower.

Take into consideration expressions to be the building blocks of communication, with every sentence determining the significance of your interactions. I suggest that you think about the impact of self-empowering language on your trajectory to freedom of speech. As opposed to the use of language that endorses restricted views, choose uplifting and motivating statements. An example would be to substitute *"I can't"* with *"I'm learning,"* in this example, the emphasis is modified from restriction to potential.

This intentional selection of statements creates an inspiration for one's empowerment. I recommend that you continue to critically analyze how generational cycles influence communication patterns. You may want to contemplate self-reflection questions again to include restricted statements like *"this is just how it is"* or *"we've always done it this way"* established in you. The solution to empowerment is to confront these phrases and replace them with language that represents resilience, progress and potential. Empowerment through speech extends beyond self-talk to how you communicate with others. Your word choices are like seeds having the capability to either suffocate or nourish.

Adopt expressions that uplift and inspire, fostering an inclusive environment in which others feel free to express their thoughts and feelings without fear of being judged. Self-reflection becomes a continuous process as you gradually start to take into account the influence of language on establishing a culture of empowerment in your interactions. *Do your expressions encourage open discourse, or do they unintentionally contribute to communication barriers?* By actively choosing a communication language that encourages, validates and supports, you become a facilitator of empowered communication. Subsequently, this will assist in your separating from the constricting communication patterns of the past. One of the most important things that you will discover on your path to self-discovery, is the fact that honest communication forms the foundation of genuine interactions. I encourage you to regard this as an interface that merges the distance between people, allowing for the free flow of ideas, feelings and points of view. The moment that you can embrace transparency represents a major break from generational communication challenges.

Strategies for Self-Mastery and Goal Persistence

The correlation between the research and the resources in this book shows the importance of self-mastery and goal persistence. The two are problem-focused primary control strategies, in predicting fewer mental disorders. These strategies involve the belief in one's capacity to direct processes and outcomes in various life domains and persevering in goal-striving despite hardships. In a nutshell, the aspects of the research suggested that effective emotion regulation and self-help strategies can contribute to reducing symptoms of anxiety and depression.

Emotion regulation is the process of developing skills to regulate and manage emotions and can be beneficial in reducing anxiety. This may involve techniques such as deep breathing, mindfulness, or engaging in activities that promote relaxation and stress reduction. Learning the skill of emotion control can help reduce worry and support a resilient outlook. Acquiring useful abilities like awareness, deep breathing, and relaxing techniques is best. This has the potential to equip you with the strategies that you need to face life's obstacles with constant gratefulness. These strategies will teach you a sense of trust and the ability to control how you feel under pressure. Emotion regulation is a skill that encourages healthier relationships and facilitates personal growth. It is an essential ingredient of emotional intelligence, with benefits extending beyond anxiety reduction. By incorporating these empowering tactics into your everyday routine, you can start a journey toward emotional resilience, improve your well-being, and live a harmonious existence. The solution is to make an organized effort to recognize and overcome these related fears and cycles. It involves an ambitious inquiry into the core causes, admitting their existence, and knowing that they do not determine one's potential. This is your opportunity to actively try to remove the limitations that limit personal freedom and growth by recognizing these tendencies.

Open communication entails fostering inclusiveness promoting an inclusive atmosphere, where people feel comfortable expressing their true selves. It differentiates from conventional interactions, which frequently include self-limitation or adhering to defined protocols. The key component to conscious communication is active listening, in which each partner takes turns leading and following. You will be appreciative of the fact that listening actively includes not only hearing words, but thoroughly comprehending the emotions, opinions and experiences underlying them. It is a shift from traditional communication patterns in which listening is frequently an involuntary effort. It would be beneficial to think about previous communication conditions influenced by generational cycles.

Were there gaps in understanding throughout conversations? Active listening breaks this trend by emphasizing comprehension over just gaining a reaction. It entails listening to fully comprehend, cultivating a climate of tolerance and laying the groundwork for lasting interactions. Unlock your potential with practical techniques that empower you to communicate more effectively. Incorporate empowered expressions, open communication and active listening into your daily interactions to break free from old patterns and transform the way you connect with others.

Tools for revolutionizing communication skills

The following strategies are powerful tools that will further enable you to build genuine connections and revolutionize your communication skills. *Positive Affirmations*: Begin and conclude your step with positive affirmations. These inspirational sentences can transform your perspective and language, creating self-empowerment. An example of this would be affirming that "I am competent in gaining progress and proactive development."

Empathy Statements: Practice utilizing empathy statements in conversations. Instead of springing to solutions, respect the emotions of others. "*I can imagine this situation is difficult for you,*" for example. "*How are you feeling about it*? "Constructive Feedback: When providing feedback, express it constructively. Instead of responding, "*You're doing it wrong,*" say, "*I appreciate your effort.*" Let us consider how we can improve this together. *Introspective Responses:* Respond to others with introspective statements that demonstrate your comprehension. "*It sounds like you're feeling overwhelmed,*" for example. "*Is that correct?*" This method promotes more in-depth conversation.

Encourage Openness: Establish an environment that promotes openness and demonstrates your openness to listen without passing judgment. Honest communication makes a difference and adds to everyone's growth and understanding. Regular Check-Ins: Make regular check-ins a part of your interactions. This might be as straightforward as asking, "*How do you feel about our interactions?" Is there anything else you'd like to communicate or improve?"* Don't just settle for mediocre interactions, this is where you have the ability. *Have you ever considered the ripple effect on your relationships, both personal and professional, when you adopt empowering language?* The way you communicate can contribute to a culture of support and understanding. Open communication plays a vital role in fostering an atmosphere where everyone feels heard and valued. The impact of this transformative approach extends beyond individual interactions to shape the collective dialogue within your sphere of influence, take control of your life, and unleash your full potential.

It is mandatory that you utilize metrics for enhanced communication. You need it to examine the validity and significance of your relationships to determine the depth of your connection. A stronger sense of connection demonstrates fulfillment in overcoming generational communication barriers. You should assess your capacity for handling arguments with mindful communication. Successful conflict resolution demonstrates an advanced method for handling challenges, without prejudice due to generational communication habits. You are now at an important juncture in which we will be gaining an in-depth exploration of your relationships. This is a criterion for your emancipation path.

You will learn to master the art of conflict resolution. It serves as a map, navigating the intricate web of generational communication obstacles which helps review the legitimacy and relevance of your relationships. I want you to further evaluate your relationships to be a means of evaluation for determining the quality and value of your connections with others. This investigation probes below the surface to examine the fulfillment received from overcoming generational challenges to communication. View your interactions as *"surges on the outermost layers of a rough sea"* Envision that beneath the waves are unknown depths that determine the genuine nature of connection. By going into these depths, you can evaluate the legitimacy of breaking free from the cycle of generational communication habits. This will enable you to communicate more effectively with others and foster growth within your relationships. You will be able to communicate more effectively with others by embracing the following strategies.

Successful Pause and Reflect: Use a pause-and-reflect method during a quarrel. Take an introspective approach, evaluate your feelings, and consider the flip side of the other party's viewpoint. This purposeful pause prohibits knee-jerk reactions established in negative generational habits. Use "I" Statements: The use of "I" statements to frame your issues, communicate your thoughts and wants without assigning blame. For example, you might say, *"I feel hurt when this happens, and I need us to find a solution together"*, this shifts the emphasis away from assertions and in favour of collaborative problem-solving. *Active Listening in Conflict: Practice* active listening to ensure you comprehend the other someone's point of view during conflicts. Absorb what they have said before answering, display empathy and a genuine desire to understand their point of view.

Seek Common Ground: Pay attention to the focus of agreement even when you don't agree. Identifying shared values or goals lays the groundwork for identifying solutions that benefit both sides. This inclusive method breaks the cycle of negative communication. Utilize Compromise: Conflict resolution frequently requires a compromise. Investigate the differences of several points of view, leading to a more powerful framework of understanding. Embrace Collective Viewpoints: Value and embrace mutual goals as common ground. This strategy forms the framework for connectedness, by emphasizing points of view that connect people, irrespective of generational differences. Think about a shared journey towards a mutually desirable conclusion, rather than an admission of weakness. This strategy supports a cooperative environment by breaking free from strict generational communication standards. You can further consider how generational communication norms shaped prior disputes. Were there instinctive responses or a reluctance to participate in discussion during the arguments?

Chapter 4

Chapter 4: Breaking Generational Cycles

How Can I identify and Break these Patterns?

Your life may be viewed as a collection of chapters; with the pages of prejudice, norms, and expectations from society. These are all a collection of experiences that may either move us forward or entangle us in tenacious threads of generational cycles. You struggle to overcome the constraints imposed by cultural complexities that sometimes function on automation. Your fears are sometimes those hidden shadows that haunt your dream. Subsequently, this may cause uncertainties in our daily lives and frequently have its roots in the soil of cultural expectations.

Your culture may cultivate a story that influences your choices, preferences, and innermost concerns. The need to fit into the norm imposed by previous generations can be overbearing at times, forcing you to live with apprehensions that seem never-ending. Examine the impact of inherited worries on decision-making and general well-being. The goal is to see this impact decrease, indicating an improvement in approach to life. Include mindfulness in your daily routine.

Scrutinize how mindfulness activities boosted your level of self-awareness and guided you on a deliberate approach to breaking free from negative generational patterns. As you continue on the path of transition, you learn to pay more attention to the microcurrents that are influencing your general health and decision-making. This chapter of your life focuses on inherited concerns, the silent decision-makers in your life, to lessen their influence. The aim is to develop a life that aligns with your fresh perspective as you courageously navigate the passageways of self-discovery. The negative patterns of your behaviour from your family's history run parallel to shady characters who subtly influence your choices and obscure your overall well-being. These could subtly control your life's path and manifest as anxieties about failure, inadequacy, or risk aversion. Look at each concern as a puzzle piece that adds to your improved mental image.

Examining these elements, comprehending their significance, and progressively lessening their influence on your way of living is the goal. The objective is to lessen the influence of worries so that you may navigate life with greater resilience and clarity, not to eliminate them which is an impractical goal. Take a moment to pause.... consider the effects of inherited concerns. It is a life-changing action, and each step demonstrates the tenacious human spirit's capacity for growth, learning, and self-discovery. Freedom is not only a personal project; it is an ongoing effort aimed at removing the fetters of generational cycles and nurturing a legacy of empowerment. Inherited phobias are the silent actors of our choices, manipulating your decisions without our knowledge.

Consider your anxieties to be shadows from the past, lingering in the depths of your mind. They are your descendants' echoing whispering doubts, anxieties and restrictions that might quietly affect your judgments. In this phase of your life, you are now establishing an effort to uncover these fundamental impacts and learn how they impact your overall well-being. The first stage of this mission is determining the extent to which these hereditary discomforts have made an impact. It is comparable to putting your decision-making process under scrutiny. *How much influence do your apprehensions have on your decisions? Do they lead gently or with steel traction?* Keeping in mind their power is not a sign of weakness it indicates brave self-awareness. It's the light you shed on the darkness, revealing the corners and crevices where these problems reside. I encourage you to be genuine with your abilities. Peel back the layers, delve deep into the reasoning behind your decisions, and don't be afraid to acknowledge your ancestral concerns. Only by facing them will you obtain the power to reduce their influence.

A decrease in the impact of inherited concerns indicates a positive adjustment in your progress. This sense of optimism is not a temporary feeling; it is a genuine sign that you are regaining control over your actions and, as a result, your life. I want you to now examine the direction that your life is taking and pause to consider a few things. *How closely do your decisions correspond with your goals rather than problems acquired from previous generations?* It's an important question, like recalibrating your internal navigation system. Decisions that coincide with personal goals indicate a developing sense of empowerment, reclaiming a sense of authority from ancestral fears.

As you progress, I encourage you to be assertive in expressing your own expertise and providing your account of events. Investigate each decision, investigate its origins, and ask yourself: *Does this decision support my objectives, hopes, and aspirations, or is it an emotional response to concerns passed down to me?* This self-interrogation is about regaining your agency in the important account of your life, not about allocating blame. Keep an eye out for the sprouting of decision-making freedom as you go on this adventure. The emergence of a leader within oneself is a characteristic of empowerment. Decision-making autonomy is a composition of self-trust, boldness, and developing knowledge of your moral compass. Applaud each occasion in which your decisions become a representation of your true self in our metaphorical classroom. It's comparable to witnessing a student tackle a challenging subject and gain confidence in their ability. Independence in decision-making is your passport to autonomy, a clear indicator that you are not only a passenger on the voyage of life, but a cognizant decisive driver. In this phase of your life where you learn to negotiate the intricate terrain of inherited phobias; realize that this path is an uphill battle of self-discovery.... not a dash.

Evaluate the amount of their influence, celebrate every reduction in their hold as a win and associate your actions with your goals to experience decision-making freedom. The sparks of self-awareness, optimism and empowered decision-making enlighten what is needed to move forward. Therefore, endorse this lesson, appreciate the journey and continue to celebrate your development. Determine the evolution of a mindset from one restricted by generational cycles to one that promotes human growth, freedom and self-determination. Assess your ability to recover from difficult situations.

Make note of any situations when resilience has increased, showing progress in overcoming the emotional burden of inherited fears. Let's be transparent for a second. *How often do you find yourself on autopilot, reacting to things in an almost preprogrammed manner?* It's as if you're running on default settings and breaking free from that cycle requires an extensive change in your decision-making approach. Intentional decisions are more than just choices; they are declarations of your autonomy as an individual. Contemplate the following: each decision you make is an advancement in your life's journey. Instead of allowing your feet to follow a known course of negative generational patterns, you can choose the trajectory that resonates with your core values, ambitions, and desires. *Reflect on this: how many times have you said yes to something because your parents, grandparents, or society expected you to?* It's time to put a halt to the habitual impulses and start making decisions that reflect your genuine self.

Your intentional decisions may often result in positive outcomes if carefully strategized. It's about pausing, thinking about your principles, and asking yourself, *"Does this choice align with who I am and where I want to go?"* It is the solution to the knee-jerk reactions bound into the substance of negative generational habits. Breaking free involves breaking the cycle, and deliberate decisions are your one-of-a-kind arsenal. You have the power to break the cycle of automatic solutions and instead choose with intention. This is a conscious decision about recovering your capacity to make conscious, clear, and honest decisions. Intentional decisions result in positive outcomes. Actions for personal development are the obvious notes in the life classroom.

As you explore the trajectory of breaking free from inherited negative patterns, study these behavioural changes with the precision of an aware learner along the pathway. You are encouraged to start to examine your emotional reactions to challenging occurrences as you break free from inherited concerns. Increased emotional resilience indicates that you are getting more competent at separating yourself from the emotional impact of generational loads. You may choose to regard emotional resilience as the ability to survive a storm without losing your inner peace. It is not about suppressing emotions, but rather about creating a balanced reaction to situations. For example, if financial failures were a trigger for excessive fear that was founded in generational patterns; watch how your emotional responses grow. You may notice a gradual shift from panic to proactive problem-solving, a sign of your building emotional resilience. Behavioural modifications serve as guideposts along your transforming path, pointing you in the direction of authenticity and freedom. These transitions are not isolated events, but rather seeds planted in your garden of personal development.

Each day you have the opportunity to discover budding plants, each adding to the developing story of your victory. As you break free, you may notice behavioural changes in numerous facets of your life. It could be your communication style, the chances you're willing to take, or the boundaries you set. Think of those times when you surprised yourself by responding differently than expected. This self-awareness serves as a compass, directing you towards more focused and powerful living. Emotional resilience is a series of actions including inner strength, adaptation and self-compassion. Imagine yourself as the lead performer, effortlessly handling life's problems with a newfound sense of balance.

The choreographic process of emotional resilience is about navigating through obstacles with grace rather than avoiding them. Examine how your emotional reactions change in the face of adversity. If a setback used to fill you with despair, you will now have a reservoir of strength within and the ability to see setbacks as opportunities for growth. Emotional resilience enables you to embrace the journey, whirling through challenges without losing your primary focus. You are now clearer about the process, therefore, the next time life throws you an unexpected challenge, hit the pause button, take a deep breath, and make a decision that you want. Intentional decisions are sometimes just rewriting the script and embracing a story that is uniquely yours, not just generating a new pattern in your life. In your daily life, attitudes may have a subtle but profound influence. Breaking negative patterns entails changing those attitudes. It's like shifting from a fixed perspective to a growth mindset, from seeing issues as hurdles to seeing them as chances for growth. You have complete command as it relates to developing an attitude that pulls you forward and remember your perspectives are the lenses through which you view the world.

Let us explore more deeply how negative patterns can be broken. Your first step in this stage is to recognize and address the need to break patterns that are no longer beneficial to your personal development. This is actively breaking free from inherited notions and striving to see the world through your perspective. Your unique experiences, values, and goals deserve an active role in developing your perception of the world. It's about giving yourself that chance to develop into a more harmonized version of yourself with your present situation. Breaking negative patterns necessitates a change in this area as well.

This may entail deliberately selecting alternate behaviours, attitudes, or viewpoints that disrupt rooted generational patterns. *Are you willing to seize the bull by the horns and shake things up?* If you're exhausted from repeating the same old song and want to break free from the bonds of negative generational patterns that have kept you hostage; you've made the ideal step. Get ready to plunge into the methodology of breaking negative patterns and paving the road for a life that is uniquely and gleefully yours. Fundamentally, disrupting patterns is not an indication of a complete redesign; rather, it entails a meticulous, purposeful change. You can think of this to be the equivalent of pressing the reset button on a computer that has been functioning on obsolete software for far too long. Breaking negative patterns takes deliberate effort, a dedication to self-discovery, and a determination to *"fight against all odds"*. It's about comprehending that the fact something has always been done a certain way is not meant to indicate it's the only or best way for you. Before you engage on this journey of breaking negative patterns, realize that it is an embodiment of progress.

This is about releasing yourself from what no longer benefits you and embracing the exciting freedom that comes with selecting a new path. You are nurturing a life that reflects the amazing, uniquely designed soul that you were designed to be. As you continue on this journey, the destination becomes more clear; the evolution of your mindset. You are breaking free from negative generational cycles; cultivating a mindset that propels you to unparalleled levels of human growth, freedom, and self-determination.

The S.O.L.V.E method is the blueprint for the path to your mental emancipation; permit it to guide you through the changes. The way we think sometimes remains connected to the limits of the past in the vacuum of generational cycles. There are times in which you may feel as if you are being held back by invisible weights. This may be constructed from anxieties and restraints passed down through unconscious generational patterns. Breaking free from this bubble warrants a deliberate and purposeful effort to move beyond the limitations that have confined the mindset for generations. Instead of viewing your current cocoon as a place of captivity, I implore you to see it as a vessel of metamorphosis ready to unfold. It's time to measure your mental progress and how far you've come from the limitations of the past to the boundless possibilities of development and emancipation. The assessment of your resilience is a key indicator of your progress. The emotional muscle that flexes and strengthens in the face of adversity is known as resilience. Consider it an untapped talent that silently evolves within you every time you recover from a challenging scenario.

How to Consciously Manage the Impact of These Negative Trends

Your inherent patterns of worries may seem like a relentless habit, tearing at the infrastructure of your ambitions. These problems frequently span generations and may result in a whirlpool of feelings relating to anxiety. *Are you ready to identify these patterns, comprehend their origins, and consciously manage generational currents?* The navigating tool of S.O.L.V.E will be that tool that you apply to cut through the maze of worries. You have the power to cultivate the empowering spirit of your path.

Allow yourself to be free of constraining notions.... those self-imposed limitations and be open to the endless possibilities. You have the S.O.L.V.E toolkit and the power to start reducing the barriers to your personal development. Remember that you are not alone while you manage the currents of inherited concerns. We all carry remnants of the past with us. The steps on this journey are small, yet filled with potential because you are armed with the S.O.L.V.E attitude. You have the toolkit to guide you and you will develop the power of evicting thoughts that constrain you. Remember that you are not alone while you manage the currents of inherited concerns. We all carry echoes of the past with us. You have unrestricted potential to embrace your journey. You can break out of the concepts that constrain you and notice that you're not only on a path to emancipation you are also creating your successful story. The primary reasons why individuals are constrained by inherited concerns and generational cycles are frequently due to the deep influence of family interactions and cultural expectations. Individuals absorb attitudes, anxieties, and behaviors exhibited by their parents and ancestors from an early age.

These established tendencies provide an intangible structure that can stifle personal development and individuality. Positive reappraisal is a type of emotion-focused secondary control that is associated with a lower prevalence of major depressive disorder (MDD), generalized anxiety disorder (GAD), and panic disorder (PD), according to a study on cognitive and behavioural methods by Nur et al. (2019). As you continue on this journey, the destination of the evolution of your mindset is more apparent. You are breaking free from generational cycles; cultivating a mindset that propels you to unparalleled levels of human growth, freedom, and unabashed self-determination. The S.O.L.V.E method is the blueprint for the path to your mental emancipation and permits you to lead you through the changes.

The way we think sometimes remains connected to the limits of the past in the vacuum of generational cycles. There are times in which feel as if you are being held back by invisible weights constructed from anxieties and restraints passed down through unconscious biological inheritance. Breaking free from this bubble warrants a deliberate and purposeful effort to move beyond the limitations that have confined the mindset for generations. As your guide on this life-changing journey, I urge you to consider the cocoon that you may be in currently as a vessel of transformation waiting to unravel, rather than a place of confinement. It's time to assess your mental evolution and quantify the distance traveled from the constraints of the past to the limitless horizons of growth and freedom. The assessment of your resilience, a key indicator of your progress, is an important part of this evolution. The emotional muscle that flexes and strengthens in the face of adversity is known as resilience. Consider it an untapped talent that silently evolves within you every time you recover from a challenging scenario. Breaking away from cultural chains is not without difficulties. To question the existing quo, you need to muster the strength to confront the probable pushback or criticism.

This process of challenging and redefining negative cultural beliefs, on the other hand, can result in personal empowerment, a more authentic sense of self, and the potential to contribute to positive societal change. Finally, the interrelationship of values and fears with cultural conditioning emphasizes the significance of individual action in determining one's beliefs and behaviours. You can be free from inherited constraints and contribute to the continual advancement of societal values by actively questioning, criticizing, and redefining deeply ingrained cultural norms

Chapter 5

Chapter 5: Importance of Tracking Progress and Personal Growth

Assessment Strategies and Progress Tracking

It is detrimental to your progress to document your improvements as you progress. Remarkably, it is those intentional steps that ultimately redefine your journey, hence please track the progress that eventually leads to a decline in negative patterns as time progresses. In this first step, I encourage you to welcome the winds of change. Embrace the S.O.L.V.E approach, which is outlined in detail to help you make international choices to shape your self-discovery and break negative patterns. Developing bravery is an intricate process.

It is vital to bear in mind that courage is the triumph over fear. In this inspirational journey, consider courage as the cognitive muscle that strengthens with every challenge encountered. Confronting your worries and uncertainties will gradually strengthen your courage, just like learning a new subject does. For you to develop effective solutions necessitates the kind of bravery you are required to tackle inherited challenges head-on.

This may be seen as a critical thinking exercise in which you deconstruct and analyze each issue, challenging its validity and impact on your development. By confronting the shadows of doubt with courage, you not only confront fears, but also create the road for significant transformation. This procedure is comparable to unlearning obsolete theories to make a place for new perspectives. Effective solutions act as intellectual tools, gradually stripping mental boundaries and freeing your mind to explore undiscovered territories of growth, learning and self-discovery. As you divulge constructive answers, you are not just changing your life script, but also engaging in significant intellectual exercise. You must find the bravery to approach concerns with the curiosity of a committed learner and allow effective answers to resound. You may think of this as solving a complicated calculation or deconstructing a thought-provoking work of literature. You may feel restricted because you have not been exposed to various ways of life.

Limited exposure minimizes the range of possibilities, maintaining existing anxieties and behaviors. Finding freedom requires seeking out new experiences, moving beyond one's comfort zone, and expanding one's perspectives. Observe challenging circumstances as chances for personal development rather than as obstacles to overcome. *When have you been more resilient and made strides toward releasing the emotional weight of ingrained fears?* It's during these times of overcoming obstacles that reveal the potential of your changing perspective. Your personal growth on this path manifests itself gradually rather than in a bold way. By making small, yet steady efforts towards personal independence and self-determination, your perspective changes.

Think of it like a staircase: every step is a victory, evidence that you can let go of fears from previous generations and proceed towards a mindset that welcomes change. Start with the practice of self-compassion and acknowledge the importance of each step you take. The accumulation of small adjustments that constitute the foundation of your changing thinking is just as important as the major turning points in your life. Knowing that every inch of growth is a success worthy of highlighting in the journey of transformation, I celebrate every stride with you. Tough circumstances serve as the building blocks for your mental sculpting rather than acting as obstacles on this excursion. It's time to reconsider how you view obstacles. These are the sculptors molding the edges of your changing perspective rather than as adversaries. When faced with hardship, consider how it can further your development. *What lessons can I learn from it?* Recognize the task at hand and actively engage in the restructuring procedure.

It's not about disregarding the challenges; rather, it's about turning your attention to the chances it presents for growth and resilience. Adversity catalyzes the development of your attitude by putting it to the test and enhancing its ability for self-determination. You could visualize your changing mentality as a piece of literature. Every phase is a dimension of your development, an arrangement that flows with the blend of your independence and autonomy. Imagine this project as a continuous collection of your chapter rather than a final product, an actual manifestation of your capability to overcome the constraints affixed to you by generational patterns.

Strive towards the goals and remember that every encounter, every difficulty, and every victory adds a different tune to the mental melody that continues to evolve. It's a collection of progress, resiliency, and unflinching faith in your ability to make your own decisions. *Importance of Smart Goals*: Make sure your goals are SMART (specific, measurable, achievable, relevant, and time-bound). A SMART goal would be, "Start one new project of transformation e.g. learning to manage the anxiety that involves an element of uncertainty within the next three months," for example, if one inherited pattern is a fear of taking risks then this level of detail turns a vague goal into a concrete action plan. Think of your growth objectives as checkpoints along the way to your transformation. These are the turning points that enhance your development. In the broader scheme of things, significant achievements turn into the summits you scale, each triumph serves as a monument of your tenacity and resolve. While pursuing transformative objectives, let's not lose sight of the small but daily victories. These are the small behavioural adjustments, the times when bravery is chosen above comfort. Respect the significance of constancy in minor victories.

Here is an example...if your goal is to break free from established patterns of self-doubt celebrate each time you speak up more in meetings. Little triumphs like these add up and create a pathway towards significant change. Every input shows how far you've come, whether it's finishing a difficult activity, tackling a fear you have, or sticking to your goals for a step. The practice not only helps to maintain optimism but also acts as a source of inspiration when things are hard. As you keep sowing the seeds of your personal growth; flexibility turns into a virtue. You are constantly evolving and so is life itself. Your personal development objectives ought to reflect flexible guidelines that change as you do, rather than inflexible rules that stop at the first hurdle.

Evaluate the relevancy of your goals as you proceed. *Do they still correspond with your changing goals?* If not, do not be afraid to graciously modify them. It's the acceptance that growth is an ongoing process and that your objectives should be flexible rather than stubborn rulers. The structure of the part of the process is to develop a regular assessment routine. Permit yourself to navigate the landscape of your emotions, thoughts, and behaviours by setting aside time for introspection. I want you to carefully reflect on this checkpoint where you pause to celebrate wins though small; analyze obstacles and re-calibrate your journey. This process is about analyzing and adjusting your existing trajectory so that your journey remains consistent with your growing goals. The efficiency of selected strategies forms the cornerstone of your growth as you travel through this adventure. Consider these strategies to be tools in your personal growth toolbox, each serving a specific role in breaking down the walls of generational cycles. Envision yourself as a skillful navigator, exploring a route toward your true character.

Positive behaviours provide the foundation of your new story as you break away from inherited cycles. Consider these habits to be the structure of your life, influencing your ideas, behaviours, and overall well-being. The daily routines that create your character and define the quality of your life are the building blocks of transformation. These are now your emancipators rather than constraints. They provide a framework that encourages progress, instills discipline and creates a good mindset. Identify habits that are in line with your goals. Dedicate yourself to a meaningful and purpose-driven existence; have positive habits, cultivate healthy routines and mindful practices. Your ultimate purpose of breaking free from negativity is to live a meaningful life.

Successful dispute resolution demonstrates your progress and evolution. Regard your conflicts not as battles won or lost, but as opportunities for growth and relationship strengthening. Evaluate the impact of conflict resolution and breaking out from generational communication habits. *Has your path equipped you to approach issues with a proactive and understanding mindset?* Successful conflict resolution becomes evidence of your advanced methods, demonstrating the paradigm-shifting potential of mindful communication. The art of mastering conflict-solving is not an easy process therefore, the following practical strategies are designed to help you navigate using mindful communication techniques. These tools may act as your navigator guiding you through the storm and breaking you free from the cycle of generational communication habits. You can foster growth within your relationships and communicate more effectively with others by embracing the following strategies.

Successful Pause and Reflect: Use a pause-and-reflect method during a quarrel. Take an introspective approach, evaluate your feelings, and consider the flip side of the other party's viewpoint. This purposeful pause prohibits knee-jerk reactions established in negative generational habits. *Use "I" Statements*: Use "I" statements to frame your issues, communicating your thoughts and wants without assigning blame. For example, you might say, "*I feel hurt when this happens, and I need us to find a solution together.*" This shifts the emphasis away from assertions and in favor of collaborative problem-solving.

Chapter 6: Tracking Progress -Goal Setting

The Importance of Smart Goal/ Goal Setting in the Process

We have already established why it is detrimental to document your improvements as you progress. Remarkably, it is those intentional steps that redefine your journey. Please track the progress that eventually leads to a decline in negative patterns as time progresses. I encourage you to welcome the winds of change.

Embrace the S.O.L.V.E approach to help you make intentional choices in shaping your self-discovery journey. Developing bravery is an intricate process; it is vital to bear in mind that courage is the triumph over fear. In this inspirational journey, consider courage as the cognitive muscle that strengthens with every challenge encountered. Confronting your worries and uncertainties will gradually strengthen your courage, just like learning a new subject does. For you to develop effective solutions necessitates the kind of bravery you are required to tackle inherited challenges head-on.

This may be seen as a critical thinking exercise, in which you deconstruct and analyze each issue; challenging its validity and impact on your development. By confronting the shadows of doubt with courage, you not only confront fears; but also create the road for significant transformation. This procedure is comparable to unlearning obsolete theories to make a place for new perspectives. Effective solutions act as intellectual tools, gradually stripping mental boundaries and freeing your mind to explore undiscovered territories of growth, learning and self-discovery. As you divulge constructive answers, you are not just changing your life script, but also engaging in significant intellectual exercise. You have to find the bravery to approach concerns with the curiosity of a committed learner and allow effective answers to resound. Think of this as similar to solving a complicated calculation or deconstructing a thought-provoking work of literature. You may feel restricted because you have not been exposed to various ways of life. Your limited exposure minimizes the range of possibilities due to existing anxieties and behaviors.

The path to freedom, requires seeking out new experiences, moving beyond one's comfort zone and expanding one's perspectives. Observe challenging circumstances as chances for personal development rather than as obstacles to overcome. *When have you been more resilient and made strides toward releasing the emotional weight of ingrained fears?* It is during these times of overcoming obstacles that reveal the potential of your changing perspective. Your personal growth on this path manifests itself gradually rather than in a bold way. By making small, yet steady efforts towards personal independence and self-determination, your perspective changes. Think of it like a staircase: every step is a victory. This is evidence that you can let go of fears from previous generations and proceed towards a mindset that welcomes change.

Start with the practice of self-compassion and acknowledge the importance of each step you take. The accumulation of small adjustments that constitute the foundation of your thinking is just as important as the major turning points in your life. Knowing that every inch of growth is a success worthy of highlighting in the journey of transformation; I celebrate every stride with you. Tough circumstances serve as the building blocks for your mental sculpting rather than acting as obstacles on this excursion. It's time to reconsider how you view obstacles. These are the sculptors molding the edges of your changing perspective rather than as adversaries. When faced with hardship, consider how it can further your development. *What lessons can I learn from it?* Recognize the task at hand and actively engage in the restructuring procedure.

It's not about disregarding the challenges; rather, it's about turning your attention to the chances it presents for growth and resilience. Adversity catalyzes the development of your attitude by putting it to the test and enhancing its ability for self-determination. Every phase is a dimension of your development, an arrangement that flows with the blend of your independence and autonomy. Imagine this project as a continuous collection of your life story rather than a final product. Strive towards the goals and remember that every encounter, every difficulty, and every victory adds a different path as you progress. It's a collection of progress, resiliency, and unflinching faith in your ability to make your own decisions.

Importance of Smart Goals

Make sure your goals are SMART (specific, measurable, achievable, relevant, and time-bound). A SMART goal would be, "Start one new project of transformation e.g. learning to manage the anxiety that involves an element of uncertainty within the next three months. For example, if one inherited pattern is a fear of taking risks, then this level of detail turns a vague goal into a concrete action plan. Think of your growth objectives as checkpoints along the way to your transformation. These are the turning points that enhance your development. In the broader scheme of things, significant achievements turn into the summits you scale, each triumph serves as a monument of your tenacity and resolve.

These are the small behavioural adjustments. Respect the significance of constancy in minor victories. Here is an example...if your goal is to break free from established patterns of self-doubt, celebrate each time you speak up more in meetings. Little triumphs like these add up and create a pathway towards meaningful change. Every input shows how far you've come, whether it's finishing a difficult activity, tackling a fear you have, or sticking to your goals for a step. The practice not only helps to maintain optimism but also acts as a source of inspiration when things are hard. As you keep sowing the seeds of your personal growth; flexibility turns into a virtue.

You are constantly evolving and so is life itself. Your personal development objectives ought to reflect flexible guidelines that change as you do, rather than inflexible rules that stop at the first hurdle. Evaluate the relevancy of your goals as you proceed. *Do they still correspond with your changing goals?* If not, don't be afraid to graciously modify them. It's the acceptance that growth is an ongoing process and that your objectives should be flexible rather than stubborn rulers. The structure of the part of the process is to develop a regular assessment routine. Permit yourself to navigate the landscape of your emotions, thoughts, and behaviours by setting aside time for introspection. I want you to carefully reflect on this checkpoint where you pause to celebrate wins though small; analyze obstacles and re-calibrate your journey. This process is about analyzing and adjusting your existing trajectory, so that your journey remains consistent with your growing goals. The efficiency of selected strategies forms the cornerstone of your growth, as you travel through this adventure. Consider these strategies to be tools in your personal growth toolbox; each serving a specific role in breaking down the walls of generational cycles. Envision yourself as a skillful navigator, exploring a route toward your true character.

Positive behaviours provide the foundation of your new story as you break away from inherited cycles. Consider these habits to be the structure of your life, influencing your ideas, behaviours, and overall well-being. The daily routines that create your character and define the quality of your life are the building blocks of transformation. These are now your emancipators, rather than constraints. They provide a framework that encourages progress, instills discipline and creates a good mindset. Identify habits that are in line with your goals. Dedicate yourself to a meaningful and purpose-driven existence; have positive habits, cultivate healthy routines and mindful practices. Your ultimate purpose of breaking free from negativity is to live a meaningful life. Successful dispute resolution demonstrates your progress and evolution. Regard your conflicts not as battles won or lost, but as opportunities for growth and relationship strengthening.

Evaluate the impact of conflict resolution and breaking out from generational communication habits. *Has your path equipped you to approach issues with a proactive and understanding mindset?* Successful conflict resolution becomes evidence of your advanced methods, demonstrating the paradigm-shifting potential of mindful communication. The art of mastering conflict-solving is not a painless process. The following practical strategies are designed to help you navigate using mindful communication techniques. These tools may act as your navigator guiding you through the storm and breaking you free from the cycle of generational communication habits.

You can foster growth within your relationships and communicate more effectively with others by embracing the following strategies.: *Successful Pause and Reflect*: Use a pause-and-reflect method during a quarrel. Take an introspective approach, evaluate your feelings, and consider the flip side of the other party's viewpoint. This purposeful pause prohibits knee-jerk reactions established in negative generational habits. *Use "I" Statements*: Use "I" *statements* to frame your issues, communicating your thoughts and wants without assigning blame. For example, you might say, "*I feel hurt when this happens* and "*I need us to find a solution together*". This shifts the emphasis away from assertions and in favour of collaborative problem-solving.

Chapter 7: Practice Gratitude

Cultivating An Attitude of Gratitude and Giving Back to Others

During your life experience, you may find that your struggles may overpower blessings, this often results in a lack of thankfulness. In this step you are encouraged to acknowledge the difficulty of feeling thankful in the presence of unfavourable outlooks and the constraint of restricted ideas. You have the power to utilize S.O.L.V.E to remove the impediments to a happy mindset.

It's a journey of self-discovery, revealing the layers of positiveness within that are waiting to bloom in an atmosphere of appreciation. As you practice thankfulness, the metrics of your journey improve gradually. You are encouraged to notice expressions of gratitude as they emerge from your growing perspective. Each acknowledgment is a measurement of your growth. Additionally, it recognizes the declining influence of limiting belief which is visible evidence of your growing capacity for gratitude. You will learn to appreciate the fact that thankfulness is more than a temporary emotion; it is a transformational force.

Cultivating it reshapes your perspective and helps you to appreciate trivial things. You live in a world that sometimes encourages negativity; thankfulness is a reminder to be appreciative. Gratitude is more than a fluctuating emotion; it is a powerful force that shapes your attitude. The cultivation of thankfulness adjusts your perspectives so that you can see value throughout each moment. In a world that is often filled with discontent, appreciation helps guide you through life's storms. This exposes the good and fosters a mindset of abundance. This intentional habit additionally improves your emotional well-being; coaching you on to a more satisfying and appreciating life journey. The insatiable search for personal greatness continues, and you are at an iconic moment: evaluating the necessity of establishing a spiritual connection. It's easy to feel disconnected from our spiritual anchors while facing life's chaos. This is a call to action to reestablish or cultivate that connection and reap numerous rewards that can be gained from spiritual fulfillment. It is essential that amid the chaos of daily life, you cultivate a spiritual connection; this is vital because this produces equilibrium.

It is an opportunity to create a sacred space for personal meditation and to hear the whispers of your soul. The results create a deeper awareness of your spiritual nature. These practices, whether tiny acts of gratitude or more extensive spiritual activities, establish a pattern of connection. *Are you ready to incorporate specific actions into your daily routine?* The S.O.L.V.E method makes it easier to include these routines, transforming them into transformative acts that nurture your spirit.

As you engage in personal introspection and rituals guided by the S.O.L.V.E process, you will experience a greater sense of spiritual fulfillment. This is your adventure: a self-discovery composition, in which the beauty of your spiritual nature unfolds, creating a great sense of fulfillment and tranquility. The establishment of a spiritual connection extends beyond individual fulfillment to a sense of being connected beyond oneself. You may think of this as achieving a higher purpose and feeling connected to something bigger. The most important aspect of this journey is the enhanced spiritual fulfillment that comes with a powerful sense of contentment and calm.

Cultivating Corporate Social Responsibility: One of the areas of progress that you are expected to improve is making room for cultivating corporate social responsibility. We now examine the transformational potential of social responsibility whilst you continue to navigate the wider discourse of progression in the development of your powerful journey.

If you are not actively involved in social causes and community well-being, you may feel distant from the significant impact you can have on society. When you cultivate the habit of being socially responsible, you are being helpful and embracing a purpose greater than yourself. You will discover that actively participating in community efforts and social causes will enrich your personal life; while being an inspiration for positive change. This trajectory helps you to move forward in realizing the collective strength to make a significant difference in your community or city. This is helpful in your journey to incorporate a sense of belonging and purpose. You have the opportunity to advance beyond personal barriers and emerge as a positive change agent.

The guidance provided through the S.O.L.V.E strategy will shape how you cultivate social responsibility. The S.O.L.V.E method will also help you to measure your impact as it relates to social responsibilities. It is essential to document your progress as you can identify improvements on this journey. You have to be intentional as an appeal for deliberate action lies at the heart of promoting social responsibility. The paradigm-shifting strategy of S.O.L.V.E is undeniably the guiding force that will help to motivate you to find significant reasons. You have the unique opportunity to be a change agent. *Can you see how this could be this one-of-a-kind opportunity to dive into the complex demands of societal needs?* In this context, the S.O.L.V.E approach is more than just a tool; it's a mindset that motivates people towards a higher goal. The measures become landmarks on the route to a legacy that goes beyond personal stories, a legacy of societal progress, compassion and a common commitment to establishing a brighter, more inclusive future.

Overcoming Trust Concerns: By now it is established that you are on a path of progression. In this part of your journey, you are required to put place an emphasis on developing trust in your intimate relationships. Your focus should lie on overcoming trust concerns and creating a climate that values open communication and honesty. The current section goes beyond simple problem-solving, to explore the rich rewards that emerge when trust becomes the foundation of your intimate relationships. This is an ongoing journey where personal empowerment is needed for the development of trust in intimate relationships. You are making a more intentional and purposeful effort to foster transparency in your intimate relationships.

Transparency forms the foundation of fostering inclusivity which allows you to communicate your thoughts, feelings, and vulnerabilities without fear of being judged. The benefits involve exploring the rich rewards that emerge when trust becomes the foundation of your intimate relationship. Recognize that you are on a purposeful venture to foster transparency in your intimate relationships. You are making room to overcome trust concerns and create a climate that values open communication and honesty. By doing this you are fostering inclusion which allows for your partner to communicate their thoughts, feelings, and vulnerabilities without fear of being judged. Maintain the use of the S.O.L.V.E method to track your improvement in relational happiness while settling your concerns. The continuous conversation becomes a source of joy, connection, and shared progress. You are also establishing a resilient partnership that will withstand life's ups and downs.

In a nutshell, developing regular communication contributes to the path to a relationship distinguished by profound emotional connection, trust, security, increased intimacy, and general well-being. This is a beautiful journey where you discover the gems hidden beneath the rewards. Each step is an affirmation of the transformative power of consistent and open communication while cultivating lasting love and connection. As your level of trust matures, your mentality evolves into one of security and reassurance As a couple, you will feel safer knowing you can count on your spouse for support, understanding, and unwavering commitment. These benefits go beyond the alleviation of trust difficulties to contribute to a healthy relationship in which both parties feel seen, heard, and cherished.

Strategies for Improving Communication

You may experience a feeling of limitation because of communication barriers that may stem from generational communication patterns. *Can you envision yourself at a defining moment, restricted by impediments to communication, and intertwined in the rules of communication across generations?* Now that you have a solution, you can take the initiative, and effect change by strategically embracing and applying the S.O.L.V.E method. You will discover that you can take control of your future and change the trajectory as it relates to how you communicate. Throughout this book, you have gained a deeper understanding of how informed decisions help you to break free from negative generational communication norms. This will be further highlighted in this section embracing mindful communication. The guidance in this book is the roadmap to developing true relationships that go beyond the surface, in line with your goal to break free. You will be able to gain a better understanding of how prioritizing honesty and intentional communication is the foundation of your game-changing approach to interactions. An important tip for nurturing mindful communication is to prioritize genuine relationships.

It would be valuable to consider evolving from a full gathering of acquaintances to a cozy circle of genuine connections. This creates depth over surface-level interactions and quantity. Ask yourself what the importance of true relationships on your path to emancipation is. Genuine connections provide comfort, understanding, and a sense of belonging. These connections serve as anchors, anchoring you in your pursuit of personal growth and breaking free from negative inherited habits. You will learn to appreciate the fact that building true connections calls for a plan based on honesty, mutual understanding and shared values.

By embracing mindful communication, you are utilizing the S.O.L.V.E blueprint for building the connection between each interaction. Every component symbolizes a vital component that contributes to the overall framework of true connections. Honesty is what forms the basis of genuine relationships, which is the firm basis upon which trust is created. Being truthful to yourself and others creates an environment in which authenticity can flourish. Communicating your thoughts, feelings, and vulnerabilities with openness allows for reciprocal honesty in your relationships. By cultivating honesty, you will unmask incredible benefits, even as this measure helps you break free from negative generational communication patterns. You will appreciate the fact that discovering honesty propels you to express your true self. An example of honesty would be; not avoiding tough conversations but embracing them even when it seems uncomfortable.

This could be analyzed as an effective framework that bridges the distance between people, generating understanding and compassion. You will discover that by appreciating and understanding others' points of view and experiences; this produces a sense of connectedness that minimizes generational communication barriers. Mutual understanding serves as a connector between individuals. I want you to now critically reflect on your breaking-free journey as it relates to communication in relationships. Think about this question:

How does comprehending the perspectives of others challenge your established assumptions? By actively seeking to understand different points of view, you can break away from the constraints of conventional communication patterns. This comprehension serves as an opportunity for genuine connections driven by empathy for others.

The cultivation of harmony in agreements may be viewed as fuel for establishing deeper partnerships. This is the foundation that forms a common sense of purpose and values. You will develop stronger connections by forming and nurturing connections, based on shared values which strengthens the authenticity of your relationships. You may view this as that strong structure that bridges the distance between people, generating understanding and compassion. At this point, you will gain a deeper understanding of others' points of view and experiences.

This fosters an atmosphere of connectedness that extends beyond generational communication constraints. The moment you started on the journey of building profound relationships, you started cultivating stronger connections and learning the art of embracing the support of others. These connections are the bedrock of personal growth, providing a supportive network that nurtures a sense of belonging while improving your mental health and well-being.

These meaningful relationships lay the foundation for lasting connections. I want you to now critically reflect on your breaking-free journey as it relates to communication in relationships. Think about this question: *How does comprehending the perspectives of others challenge your established assumptions?* By actively seeking to understand different points of view, you can break away from the constraints of conventional communication patterns. This comprehension serves as an opportunity for genuine connections driven by empathy for others. The cultivation of harmony in agreements may be viewed as fuel for establishing deeper partnerships. This could be considered as the foundation that comes together to form a common sense of purpose and values.

You can develop stronger connections by forming and nurturing connections based on shared values; this strengthens the authenticity of your relationships. You may view this as that structure that bridges the distance between people, generating understanding and compassion. You will gain a deeper understanding of others' points of view and experiences which fosters an atmosphere of connectedness. This extends beyond generational communication constraints. The moment you started on the journey of building profound relationships, you started cultivating stronger connections.

These connections are the bedrock of personal growth, providing a supportive network that nurtures a sense of belonging while improving your mental health and well-being. These meaningful relationships lay the foundation for lasting connections, contributing to a more enriching life journey. The exchange of support within these connections not only enhances the overall quality of life but also establishes a cornerstone for emotional and psychological resilience.

If you can prioritize these aspects, this becomes a guiding principle, shaping a fulfilling path through the intricate landscape of personal connections. This is where you gain a deeper understanding of others' points of view and experiences. This fosters an atmosphere of connectedness that extends beyond generational communication constraints. The moment you started on the journey of building profound relationships, you started cultivating stronger connections and learning the art of embracing the support of others. By this time, you would have been familiar with the fact that measurement of progress is essential to the S.O.L.V.E method. You will continue to effect change by following the suggested S.O.L.V.E technique, and assess your communication skills as you progress.

In addition, you will be able to quantify the degree of success by assessing the resilience of your relationship. You will discover that you can establish real connections and break old communication patterns. The following strategies are uniquely designed to help you learn how to communicate more effectively: *Introspective Communication*: Before answering, pause to consider your thoughts and feelings rather than reverting to a conventional answer. Engage in introspective expression that corresponds with your real self. *Competence of Active Listening*: Improve your ability to listen with intent so that you are not just hearing words but also completely understand the feelings and viewpoints behind them. This mastery will help to promotes true connections as a result of exhibiting your commitment to understanding others. *Empathy as a*

Navigation Guide: Use empathy as your guide while having conversations; consider the emotions and experiences of others when replying. This deliberate approach helps establish bonds of connectedness through validating other points of view.

Inclusive Questions or Open-ended questions: Enabling thoughtful responses helps to foster deeper connections. Instead of seeking approval, investigate the differences in other points of view, leading to a more powerful framework of understanding. *Embrace Collective Viewpoints:* Value and embrace mutual goals as common ground. This strategy forms the framework for connectedness by emphasizing points of view that connect people, irrespective of generational differences, to a more enriching life journey. The exchange of support within these connections not only enhances the overall quality of life but also establishes a cornerstone for emotional and psychological resilience.

If you can prioritize these aspects, this becomes a guiding principle, shaping a fulfilling path through the intricate landscape of personal connections. You may discover that this is just not important for individual development. It is advisable to develop an understanding and appreciation of the perspectives of rooted beliefs. If previous patterns were based on adhering to cultural standards, seeking connections with similar ideals becomes revolutionary. It's about finding a circle of fellow human beings who understand your break-free path and share your vision for living with purpose. When you acknowledge the power of making informed choices before responding this serves as a pause button that allows you to consider the impact of your words. This is a significant improvement as opposed to reacting impulsively, this intentional pause encourages thoughtful replies, which aids in the process of breaking free from communication barriers. You are now evolving further on the trajectory that gently nudges you to assess previous communication practices impacted by generational norms. *Were the reactions pre-programmed and prompted by inherited scripts?*

This is where your proactive decision-making modifies these patterns. It's about choosing words that reflect your true personality, directing conversations away from predetermined responses and towards genuine communication. If you can utilize the strategy of establishing deliberate decision-making, this will also foster genuine relationships with people. You may regard this as a process of bridging the gap, where each intentional word deepens the connections of comprehension. You are then able to create a space for meaningful discourse by pausing and pondering on your comments. This will help you build relationships that transcend generational boundaries and take into account how relationships improve when deliberate communication takes predominance.

Your conversations increasingly become more significant when they are authentic, rather than using conventional templates. Your network will start to notice and take into consideration your improved communication approach. This will create a ripple effect that encourages openness and real expression. You will actualize the benefits of this, as you prioritize authentic relationships and incorporate deliberate communication into your life. The ripple effect generates a wave of change that transforms not only individual connections but also the collective discussion within your scope of influence. Your emancipation path extends its impact, inspiring others to challenge deeply entrenched communication standards and embrace authenticity. Contemplate how your actions will affect your close connections, network, community as well as future generations. Your dedication to authentic connections serves as an example of emerging away from communication patterns that impose restrictions. Pledge your dedication to true relationships, embracing honesty, mutual understanding, and shared ideals.

As you reflect on this journey, visualize creating your revolutionary communication philosophy. Commit to incorporating thoughtful decision-making into all interactions, transforming conversations into a form of expression that symbolizes emancipation path. Your philosophy functions as an affirmation of your commitment to meaningful connections and true self-expression. It reflects the revolutionary attitude of breaking free from inherited communication standards. This resolve is the way for a life full of true interactions and meaningful interaction. Let's look at some practical ways to include purposeful communication in your regular interactions.

Consider these to be tools in your breaking-free toolkit, each designed to support your progress towards authentic connection-conscious Pause...take a conscious pause before responding in a conversation. This brief pause allows you to examine the impact of your remarks. *"Is this response true to my authentic self?"* you should ask yourself. *"Does it help to create a genuine connection?"* One of the fundamental principles of personal development is to motivate people to act decisively rather than to stand by and let issues happen. The fact that you can actively face and resolve challenging circumstances increases your self-efficacy. You will then develop strong problem-solving abilities, and deeply empowers you. Your proactive approach in addition to transforming obstacles into chances for development. This fosters an attitude that values accountability and initiative. When you take decisive actions; you not only overcome obstacles, but also gain the ability to better control your destiny and bring about positive life changes. The ability to assume responsibility spurs your personal development and moves you closer to a stronger, more independent life.

Developing positive relationships is important for making connections and accepting help and support from others. Building and nurturing positive relationships can contribute to personal development by providing a support system. This fosters a sense of belonging, and promoting emotional well-being source American Psychological Association (2011)

Reflective Listening You will learn the art of reflective listening, which is a technique in which you not only hear, but also fully understand the speaker's point of view. Reflection is necessary in the ongoing journey to clarify your journey towards fostering meaningful partnerships. By acknowledging and reaffirming the other person's experience, this intentional listening builds a stronger relationship. You may view this from the angle of alignment of values, where you identify and communicate your basic values. This is where you start to incorporate these beliefs into your speech, ensuring that your words are consistent with the values that matter. *Empathy exercises* are another technique in which you learn to cultivate empathy by engaging in activities that enhance your knowledge of the feelings and experiences of others. This empathetic perspective improves your ability to respond compassionately and sincerely, allowing you to break free from generational communication habits.

You are encouraged to maintain a communication log to take note of your intentional decisions and their consequences. Reflect on the times when thoughtful decision-making resulted in more meaningful interactions. *Open communication* is about fostering a secure space for people to express their true selves. It differentiates from conventional interaction conventions, which frequently include self-limitation or adhering to defined protocols. The key component of conscious communication is active listening in which each partner takes turns leading and following.

You will be appreciative of the fact that listening actively includes not only hearing words, but thoroughly comprehending the emotions, opinions, and experiences underlying them. It is a shift from traditional communication patterns, in which listening is frequently an involuntary effort. It would be beneficial to think about previous communication conditions influenced by generational cycles. *Were there gaps in understanding throughout the conversations?*

Active Listening breaks this trend by emphasizing comprehension over just gaining a reaction. It entails listening to fully comprehending and cultivating a climate of tolerance and laying the groundwork for lasting interactions. Unlock your potential with practical techniques that empower you to communicate more effectively. Incorporate empowered expressions, open communication, and active listening into your daily interactions to break free from old patterns and transform the way you connect with others. The following strategies are powerful tools that will further enable you to build genuine connections and revolutionize your communication skills and hear someone's point of view during conflicts. Absorb what they have said before answering, displaying empathy and a genuine desire to understand their point of view. *Seek Common Ground:* Pay attention to the focus of agreement, even when you don't agree. Identifying shared values or goals, lays the groundwork for identifying solutions that benefit both sides. This inclusive method breaks the cycle of negative communication. *Utilize Compromise:* Conflict resolution frequently requires compromise. Think about a shared journey towards a mutually desirable conclusion, rather than an admission of weakness. This strategy supports a cooperative environment by breaking free from strict generational communication standards.

You can further consider how generational communication norms shaped your prior disputes. *Were there instinctive responses or a reluctance to participate in discussion during the arguments? Inclusive Communication* One of the pros of an inclusive network for those navigating the professional landscape is that it extends to professional forums. Fostering inclusive networks may be an exploration of the vibrant network that emerges when you deliberately nurture connections from diverse backgrounds. You will establish various interactions that may span across cultural, social, and professional spheres. This is done by embracing diversity as your connections may be from different backgrounds, beliefs, religions etc.

The fact that you are willing to embrace connections from various cultures is the foundation for inclusive connections. These engagements may extend beyond mere participation to actively listening, learning, and contributing to collectively shared experiences. Additionally, you may feel motivated to engage in community-based activities that extend outside of your personal network. The role of the S.O.L.V.E method within the context of measuring not just the number of new connections, but the qualitative expansion of personal network. You may keep track of your particular journey by monitoring the increasing depth of their network; noting instances in which you have embraced inclusivity. You may also track the numerous times in which you have participated in inclusive activities and actively interacted with diverse populations. Your primary goal is not simply to make contacts, but to build genuine connections that demonstrate a commitment to inclusivity. The S.O.L.V.E method will guide you to be respectful of opposing ideas, challenge your assumptions, remove biases etc.

Each new relationship adds a distinct dimension to your network, making the ongoing journey more fulfilling. The fundamental concept of fostering inclusive networks is actively pursuing interactions that are from a diverse background. By effectively utilizing the S.O.L.V.E method, you will be able to be successful in your trajectory. This path is an incubator for establishing intentional connections and nurturing meaningful interactions. Some of the mechanisms include actively participating in discussions, sharing insights, fostering collaboration, and using inclusive techniques in team-building exercises. Subsequently, by constructively fostering inclusive networks; the yield will result in a network of connections that is authentic. You will be capable enough to cultivate inclusive interactions from the diverse network of people you may interact with.

Techniques for Cultivating and Maintaining an Attitude of Gratitude To be mindful is not just a catchphrase; it's an intentional habit that encourages you to live in the present moment. You could view this as a mental workout that improves your capacity to recognize thoughts without becoming immersed in them. Simple mindfulness exercises include grounding yourself in the present moment, paying attention to your thoughts without passing judgment and practicing mindful breathing. It's important to face issues actively with a level head rather than attempting to run away from them. By engaging in mindfulness practices, you can develop your ability to observe and separate yourself from your worries. You select deliberate actions over reactive ones. Mindfulness increases self-awareness, so you can observe your thoughts fluctuations without losing yourself. When you practice mindfulness, you gain insight into your inherent worry patterns.

You will learn to see them as simply momentary clouds in the vast sky of your consciousness. Building up more self-awareness is essential to gaining asylum. By adhering to mindfulness practices, you recognize your anxieties and learn to separate from them. This frees up time to make thoughtful, deliberate decisions. It's an uplifting trip where self-awareness serves as a torch, to help you navigate the maze of destructive ancestral traditions. Mindfulness involves making deliberate choices regarding your reactions, as opposed to acting on an instinctive level due to established fears. You can master the art of conscious decision-making through mindfulness, where each decision is a step closer to living a free and independent life.

Establish personal development goals that reflect progress in overcoming inherited fear. Recognize the little accomplishments as markers of progress on your transformative journey. Envision this chapter as a blueprint that will lead you to your goals of personal growth. Celebrate your progress regularly and acknowledge the ongoing need for self-awareness. Embrace an interpersonal shift designed specifically for you, going above traditional norms, and witness your unique conversational proficiency improve. Your journey is a personal story of achievement and growth, and this book will be your guide through each phase of your journey. As you nurture the positive patterns necessary for your transforming journey, you may be faced with a challenge: the weight of parental judgments and the load of expectations from past generations. I want you to envision yourself standing beneath the weight of parental expectations in the ethos of personal transformation narratives. We are now taking a more in-depth look at the transforming impact of the S.O.L.V.E method. It is time to reclaim the charge of your identity by constructing a tale that connects with your genuine self and encourages the development of self-awareness.

Rewriting your personal story is growth which is essential to your personal development. Maintain that journal and note the intimate details of your development. Capture occasions when you become more self-aware and when you reject cultural demands to be authentic. This is not just about rewriting your story; it is also about celebrating your accomplishments. Therefore, on this important date, start to rewrite your story. Take hold of your identity and embrace the power of the S.O.L.V.E method. You will have the opportunity to let your record of events become an affirmation of the achievements of self-awareness and authenticity. Your progress will be more than just another building block in the construction of your strong, true self.

Encourage Openness: Establish an environment that promotes openness and demonstrates your openness to listen without passing judgment. This might be as straightforward as asking, *"How do you feel about our interactions?" Is there anything else you'd like to communicate or improve?"* Don't just settle for mediocre interactions. *Have you ever considered the ripple effect on your relationships, both personal and professional, when you adopt empowering language?* The way you communicate can contribute to a culture of support and understanding. Open communication plays a vital role in fostering an atmosphere where everyone feels heard and valued. *Positive Affirmations:* Begin and conclude your step with positive affirmations. These inspirational sentences can transform your perspective and language, creating self-empowerment. An example of this would be affirming that "I am competent in gaining progress and proactive development."

Empathy Statements: Practice utilizing empathy statements in conversations. Instead of springing to solutions, respect the emotions of others. "I can imagine this situation is difficult for you," for example. "How are you feeling about it?" *Constructive Feedback:* When providing feedback, express it constructively. Instead of responding, "You're doing it wrong," say, "I appreciate your effort." Let us consider how we can improve this together. Introspective Responses: Respond to others with introspective statements that demonstrate your comprehension. "It sounds like you're feeling overwhelmed," for example. Is that correct?" This method promotes more in-depth conversation.

Chapter 8

Chapter 8: Embracing Self Discovery

Understanding Your Path to Self-Discovery

Personal growth actions are the visible notes in the classroom of life. As you explore the trajectory of breaking free from inherited negative patterns, study these behavioural changes with the precision of an aware learner along the pathway. You are encouraged to start to examine your emotional reactions to challenging occurrences as you break free from concerns. Increased emotional resilience indicates that you are getting more competent at separating yourself from the emotional impact of generational loads. You may regard emotional resilience as the ability to survive a storm without losing your inner peace. It is not about suppressing your emotions, but rather about creating a balanced reaction to situations.

You may notice a gradual shift from panic to proactive problem-solving, a sign of your building emotional resilience. Behavioural modifications serve as guideposts along your transforming path, pointing you in the direction of authenticity and freedom. These transitions are not isolated events, but rather seeds planted in your garden of personal development. Each day, you have the opportunity to discover budding plants, each adding to the developing story of your release. As you break free, you may notice behavioural changes in numerous facets of your life. It could be your communication style, the chances you're willing to take, or the boundaries you set. Think of those times when you surprised yourself by responding differently than expected. This self-awareness serves as a compass, directing you towards more focused and powerful living. Emotional resilience is a series of actions including inner strength, adaptation and self-compassion. Imagine yourself as the lead performer, effortlessly handling life's problems with a newfound sense of balance.

The choreographic process of emotional resilience is about navigating through obstacles with grace rather than avoiding them. Examine how your emotional reactions change in the face of adversity. If a setback used to fill you with despair, notice if you now have a reservoir of strength. Resilience increases the ability to see setbacks as opportunities for growth. Emotional resilience enables you to embrace your challenges without losing your primary focus. The development of positive behaviour and emotional resilience will produce ripple effects that impact every aspect of your well-being. Reflect on this ripple effect to as the framework that assists in modifying the structure of your life... mental, emotional, and social.

As you progress, examine the influence of your changing behaviours on your mental health. *Do you feel empowered, as if you have control over your choices?* Take note of how enhanced emotional resilience transcends emotional well-being and permeates your relationships. Genuine connections bloom when you reply to others from a place of strength rather than emotional distress. Reflective techniques can help you interpret behaviours and create emotional resilience. These practices function as mirrors, helping you to see the intricacies of your inner world. They offer a safe space for self-awareness, which is essential to your transformational journey. Journaling is a form of reflection that is required on this journey. You must document instances of behavioural alterations and emotional responses regularly. This technique not only increases self-awareness but also serves as a documentation of your progress, a tangible witness to your liberation path. *What caused these changes? How did you get around them?*

Regular Confirmation entails frequent assessment, enables the identification of potential problem areas. It allows you to modify techniques based on what works best for you in breaking free from problems. Frequent assessment may also serve as a form of reflective thinking depending on the method chosen. Taking the time to assess progress promotes self-awareness and a better knowledge of how transformation works. Validating personal advancement is an acknowledgment of one's development. It helps to cement the idea that your trajectory is about evolving into a more empowered version of yourself. As outlined in the S.O.L.V.E method, regular evaluation allows you to constantly alter your tactics. It is the realization that breaking free is a dynamic process that requires adaptability.

Consider fine-tuning your techniques based on what works best for you, similar to modifying a ship's sails to manage changing winds. Consider the methods you've used to overcome genetic difficulties. *Have you discovered a deeply satisfying relaxation practice?* Or a goal-setting technique that motivates you? Regular evaluation forces you to tweak and improve these strategies, making them more personalized and effective. Frequent evaluation is a type of reflective thinking. Imagine reflective thinking as turning on the light in a previously dark room. It's about getting perspective on your journey, comprehending the different aspects of your actions, and decoding the technicalities of your emotional response. Pause to think of a reflective moment in which you consider a recent decision or behavioural change. Analyze why you made that decision and how it relates to your break-free path. Reflective thinking is not about judgment but understanding. The technique of asking probing questions peels back the layers of your intentions, revealing the underlying patterns at work. You cannot underestimate the dynamic power of learning how to cultivate resilience on your path to self-discovery.

Throughout this life-changing path using the S.O.L.V.E method, it is possible that you could discover previously hidden qualities and capabilities. This trajectory has refining qualities that will possibly lead you to a more inspired existence. Through purposeful engagement with personal obstacles, people discover hidden potential and acquire valuable insights into their resilience. This relentless commitment to personal growth creates the way for a richer, more powerful life in which every obstacle serves as a platform for a more genuine and content life. The key that unlocks the door to transformation is self-awareness.

Frequent assessment fosters self-awareness by allowing you to intentionally reflect on your thoughts, behaviours, and emotions. Your increased level of thinking may now allow you to view self-awareness as a constant dialogue with yourself in which you ask yourself questions like, *"Why did I react this way?"* or *"What underlying belief influenced my decision?"* You strengthen this dialogue by assessing yourself regularly and getting insights into the heart of your being. If you're attempting to break away from ancestral habits of perfectionism, self-awareness helps you to notice instances when this inclination manifests itself. Reflective thinking allows you to investigate the fundamental causes and change your techniques, resulting in a better knowledge of your tendencies. Recognizing progress is more than simply a pat on the back; it's a powerful motivation that propels you onward. The process of frequent assessment provides a transforming loop, a continual cycle of assessment, reflection, and validation. It may be seen as a continual momentum that pulls you ahead on your route to emancipation. This feedback cycle ensures that you remain interested, adaptive, and motivated as you progress through the stages of personal development.

You may regard this recognition to be a motivating soundtrack playing in the background of your trip. *"You're on the right track; keep going,"* says the encouraging voice. Acknowledge and celebrate this accomplishment, no matter how minor it appears. This acknowledgment promotes confidence that your efforts are bearing fruit, which fuels your desire to persevere. Reflect on this loop as being similar to a dynamic river, ever flowing and carving its route through your life's environment. The current that guides the flow of your thoughts and behaviours is reflective thinking.

Progress validation acts as a fruitful bank, fostering the development of your self-awareness and personal empowerment as you invest. It's also about focusing the spotlight on issues or problem areas that once exposed, become opportunities for progress. It's a courageous exploration of the aspects that need evaluation and development. Envision the impact of this behaviour on your journey to freedom. *Is it impeding your growth, or does it indicate a more fundamental underlying belief?* This internal reflection reveals potential problem areas, prompting you to adjust your strategies and induce transformation. You must incorporate introspection into your routine to harness its transforming power. Think about it a necessary part of your morning or evening routine, similar to brushing your teeth or exercising. The regularity of your contemplation becomes the structure that supports your road to freedom. For example, if mornings are your time for reflection, spend a few minutes writing down your intentions for the forthcoming step and reflecting on the behaviours or patterns you would like to notice. Return to these observations in the late afternoon, acknowledging successes and identifying growth opportunities. This discipline not only strengthens self-awareness, but also grounds your efforts to break free to intentional living.

The language you use in self-evaluation is important. Adopt a vocabulary of growth that defines challenges as opportunities and setbacks as learning opportunities. You may view this vocabulary adjustment as altering the narrative of your emancipation journey. This will help you redefine difficulties as building a mindset that thrives on constant change. Instead of saying, "*I failed at this,*" you could say, "*I've learned something valuable from this experience.*" This shift in vocabulary offers you the ability to face setbacks with exploration and resilience. It transforms setbacks into growth motivations, integrating your inner dialogue with the hope of emancipation.

Celebrating progress is a profound accomplishment that resonates throughout your entire body. You develop a sense of accomplishment and an inflow of positive emotions, including pride, excitement, and a deep sense of fulfillment. It has an emotional impact that acts as a motivator, encouraging you towards success. Take into account a moment of progress recognition in which you reflect on an important behavioural adjustment. Feel the sense of accomplishment flourish in your chest, the warmth of excitement streaming through your veins. This emotional impact is not temporary; it remains engraved in your mind, providing an element of enthusiasm during a difficult period. The following are three examples of how SMART goals can be analyzed, whether for daily or to target a specific problem within a specific timeframe. SMART *goals* are essential for your transformative reflection. Reflect on this strategy for maximizing the potential of frequent assessment in your route to freedom. Strive to take these exercises to the next level by making them Specific, Measurable, Achievable, Relevant, and Time-bound goals helps you to fulfill important achievements.

By establishing SMART goals, for example using a daily progress journal, you achieve benefits such: Specify: the ability to specify the problems/elements you wish to track in your daily progress log. For example, if you're working on overcoming a fear of rejection, identify behaviours such as voicing your opinion in a meeting or establishing a conversation with a coworker. Measurable: Keep track of your progress. Instead of a general goal like "reduce fear of rejection," focus on specific activities. Keep track of how many times you spoke up or engaged in social situations. This quantitative feature ensures that you can measure your progress accurately.

Achievable: Set achievable daily goals. Consider your schedule and obligations. If you want to jot down incidents, set aside a specified period for each step period so that it doesn't overwhelm you. Achievable objectives foster confidence and momentum. Relevant: Make sure your daily progress corresponds to your break-free goals. If your goal is to overcome social anxiety, ensure that the behaviours you notice and remark on are pertinent to this goal. Time-bound: Set aside a specified amount of time for each step of reflection. A time-bound commitment, whether it's five minutes before bedtime or during your morning coffee, gives structure and regularity to your practice. Another example would be to use reflections using SMART goals.

Specific: Outline the main point of your reflection. It could be analyzing behavioural patterns or comprehending the factors that influenced your emotional responses. Specify the areas that you intend to investigate Measurable: Establish measurable outcomes for your step-by-step reflection. Calculate the number of patterns or trends you hope to identify. If you're changing strategy, quantify the changes you intend to make based on your insights. Achievable: Maintain a moderate level of reflection goals. Don't overburden yourself with too many goals. Prioritize a few significant issues that are relevant to your break-free path to ensure a thorough understanding and practical outcomes. Relevant: Make sure your reflections are in line with the overall goal of breaking free from inherited negative patterns. If you're focusing on work-related behaviours, be sure they help you achieve your overall objective of personal and professional development. Time-bound: Establish a timetable for your step-by-step reflection routine.

Creating an established period, whether it's an hour on Sunday evening, or first thing Monday morning. This following provides you with an example of how to schedule a monthly milestone celebration: Specific: Make a list of the milestones you want to commemorate. These could be individual accomplishments, watershed moments, or consistent growth in key areas. Be specific about what you consider to be a milestone. Measurable: Establish criteria for your goals. Measurable criteria provide precision to your celebrations, whether it's accomplishing a certain number of difficult activities or maintaining great behaviours for a set period. Achievable: Make sure your monthly goals are attainable. While huge accomplishments are motivating, concentrating on goals that are actually within reach. This helps to keep you motivated and gives you a sense of success. Relevant: Align your monthly celebrations with your goals for breaking free. If your overall goal is to build emotional resilience, make sure your milestones show success in this area. Time-bound: It could be the last step of the month or a particular step that has meaning for you. A time-bound celebration provides structure and anticipation to your journey.

You can develop SMART goals for specific problem areas: Specific: Define the problem area you want to investigate. Whether it's a specific inherited pattern, a reoccurring dilemma, or particularly restricting behaviour, define the issue you want to S.O.L.V.E . Measurable: Quantify your research. It may entail tracking instances or patterns associated with the specified problem area. For example, if impatience is a problem, count the number of times impatience appears. Achievable: Keep your exploring objectives in check. Choose one problem area to investigate at a time, ensuring that you can devote enough focus and reflection to get valuable insights.

Relevant: Make sure the problem area you investigate is relevant to your break-free objectives. If impatience is hindering your success, your investigation should be beneficial to conquering this inherited challenge. Timebound: Set a time limit for your problem area. A deadline, whether it's a step or a specified number of steps, creates an urgency to the investigation, stimulating focused and routine thought. By using SMART criteria in your transformative reflection exercises, you add intention and structure to your break-free journey. These goals serve as the framework that accelerates you toward self-awareness, personal evolution, and meaningful achievements. Here is where I guide you further in understanding the underlying power of establishing: self-mastery, goal persistence, and positive reappraisal. These are all cognitive and behavioral strategies that can contribute to your emotional well-being. The process of engaging in cognitive restructuring through the recommended guide will allow for substantial changes in your mental landscape.

This is an effective strategy that allows you to focus on and eliminate negative or unreasonable thinking, promoting a realistic and positive mindset. You will be able to achieve mastery over anxiety by proactively noticing and modifying these negative thought patterns, creating an atmosphere of improved well-being. Cognitive restructuring is more than just changing one's thoughts; it is a path of self-discovery and empowerment. By challenging and reshaping your mental framework, you establish the groundwork for long-term beneficial transformation. Each modified idea is an achievement towards becoming a more resilient, optimistic and fulfilled version of yourself. Therefore, grasp cognitive restructuring's refining power to establish avenues to improved cognitive focus and personal fulfillment Nur et al (2019).

It takes a conscious decision to start the transformational path by releasing yourself from the limitations imposed by social norms. The S.O.L.V.E technique helps break through generational constraints and cultivate inner confidence. Inner confidence is where personal empowerment begins. This route is significant because it's a deliberate step towards emancipating yourself from other people's expectations. This procedure provides you with specific guidance for navigating the complex terrain of confidence intertwined with family expectations. Cultivating self-assurance and empowerment is the goal, and the ground-breaking S.O.L.V.E method is an inspiring invitation to break free from social conventions. Breaking away from cultural chains is not without difficulties. To question the existing status quo: you need to muster the strength to confront the probable criticism. This process of challenging and redefining cultural beliefs, on the other hand, can result in personal empowerment, a more authentic sense of self, and the potential to contribute to positive societal change.

Finally, the interrelationship of values and fears with cultural conditioning emphasizes the significance of individual action in determining one's beliefs and behaviours. You can free yourself from inherited constraints. You can advance beyond societal values by actively questioning, criticizing, and redefining deeply ingrained cultural norms. Throughout the contents of this book, you will witness the complex association of acquired behaviours established by generations. Let's proceed into the S.O.L.V.E Method, a framework that empowers you to overcome the deeply entrenched patterns imprinted by your lineage, chapter by chapter.

According to the article by Palmer (2020), you accumulate insights into the complexity of developing habits as time progresses. This will analyze learned associations and provide insight on how the learned patterns produce lasting traces of your behaviour. This path to self-discovery explores the unnoticed connections that exist between those acquired behaviours and the way you communicate. While the primary focus of the article was on habits and their modification, it was also utilized to compare the ways in which parental behaviours impact communication patterns that are based on learned habits. The S.O.L.V.E Method described in this book will help you through the challenging task of breaking free from the bonds of negative generational cultural norms. As you peruse throughout the pages of this book, the underlying matter of modifying ingrained patterns appears. You will gradually grow more aware of how to modify your communication habits to disconnect yourself from the negative shadows of your family's past. This allows for self-reflection, allowing you to recognize the pervasive power of learned associations and habits and urging you to break free.

Communication is an extremely complex path in the landscape of your development. The S.O.L.V.E Method is your key to the disintegration of each of these components and actively reestablishing your communication patterns. It's a path that encourages you to enthusiastically embrace adventure, unlock personal growth, and break free from restrictions. Societal expectations, customs, and prejudices generate a network that can imprison individuals in generational cycles. Fears frequently stem from a need to adhere to cultural expectations, whether consciously or subconsciously.

Breaking these bonds entails critically assessing society's standards, embracing individualism, and challenging societal expectations that no longer support personal growth. Sometimes, you may imagine life to be like a collection of chapters, with the strands of prejudice, norms, and expectations from society. It's like a collection of experiences that may either move us forward or entangle us in tenacious threads of generational cycles. You CAN break free, and overcome the constraints imposed by cultural complexities that sometimes function on automation. Your fears are sometimes those hidden shadows that haunt your dreams subsequently this may cause uncertainties in our daily lives and frequently have their roots in the soil of cultural expectations. Your culture may cultivate a story that influences choices, preferences, and innermost concerns. The need to fit into the norm imposed by previous generations can be overbearing at times, forcing you to live with apprehensions that seem never-ending. But here's the exciting news: you can break free from the unseen bonds that anchor you to defunct accepted practices. It all starts with a bold act of self-reflection and an unshakable desire to call the fundamental structure of society standards into question.

It's about asking the question that matters most: "*Is this expectation serving my growth, or is it merely a relic of the past, handed down like an heirloom without consideration for its relevance to my unique journey?* "Breaking free demands an unrelenting discovery of your individuality. It's about accepting the inconsistencies, passions, and dreams that make you uniquely you. It's a call to arms, a declaration that deviating from a conventional is not only acceptable but phenomenal. Your path to autonomy entails fearlessly accepting the events of your life and an unwavering determination to live life on your terms. Let us now discuss exceeding societal expectations.

You are a warrior wielding the sword of critical thought, society's expectations may have once felt impassable, but empowered with the tenacity to challenge, you become an unstoppable force. You are not being rebellious, you are developing foresight, you are sifting through the various layers of history and rejecting what no longer adds value to the decision-making pattern of your ambitions. Remember that your path to breaking free is not a single undertaking. It's an integrated transformation in which one's act of resistance helps to shift societal expectations. By questioning the existing normal, you not only empower yourself but also emerge as a torch for those seeking the bravery to embark on their road of self-discovery. In a nutshell, the route of breaking free from generational cycles and cultural expectations is a celebration of your uniqueness. You will learn to nurture your inner strength, challenge the narratives that have been negatively imposed on you, and establish a path that resonates with your own passions. The world will be waiting to meet your true, emancipated self.

You have the arsenal in which the transformational power of S.O.L.V.E helps to spearhead your communication journey as you set out to shape your destiny. You will learn the importance of creating real connections rather than to just breaking down existing barriers. You will appreciate authentic relationships and experience the process in which empowered communication emerges. Each step of the journey that you experience a breakthrough in communication ultimately becomes a stride towards the future that you want. A prevalent issue that you may face involves: being confined by generational cycles that obstruct personal milestones. You have the opportunity to be free from being trapped in the clutches of generational cycles that may restrain you from achieving your milestone.

You are now able to escape constricting concepts using S.O.L.V.E as an aid to overcome barriers as you set and achieve personal goals. It is an inevitable victory once you apply the transformative S.O.L.V.E method in the process. *Are you able to visualize yourself breaking free from the constraints that inhibit your individual growth by the bonds of generational cycles?* You have the power to evade limiting concepts. S.O.L.V.E is your tool to overcome barriers as you set and achieve personal goals. Contemplate these negative concepts to be invisible chains of restrictions that have kept you back. I want you to affirm your emancipation statement, affirming that you can break free from these bonds. You have already accepted the invitation to address self-imposed limitations, cultural expectations, and inherited ideas. Recognize that boundaries exist only in your mental capacity. You are now at an important juncture; break free from the shroud of comfort since transformation takes root in discomfort.

If you can acknowledge the limiting ideas that have silently guided your decisions, then you are at a pivotal moment of self-awareness, a necessary step before breaking free. Remember, as you challenge these limiting notions, courage becomes an alliance Be ready to accept discomfort as the furnace in which your courage is created. As you progress on your transformative journey, here lies another challenge: self-doubt intertwined with the usual framework of family-related turmoil. You have an opportunity to establish a triumph rather than just a continuation. Imagine yourself battling self-doubt and the repeated turmoil of family-related issues in the repetitions of personal narratives.

The course of action for the step is the balancing resonance of the S.O.L.V.E method. It is more than just an acronym; it is the master key to the trajectory of your life. If you can use this method to reshape your tactics, you have the power to break free from the discord of self-limiting beliefs and resolute habits woven into generational traditions. Let us examine some of these indicators. Identifying wins is critical to the topography of your victory. During this step, use it as your guide. It is recommended that you acknowledge, and more importantly, celebrate victories over limiting beliefs. It is not just about breaking free from generational traditions; it is about raising your level of accomplishment to a new height. Thus, let us consider direct coherence in this spectacular step. Embrace the power of S.O.L.V.E, learn how to overcome self-limiting ideas. Each victory is an accompaniment in the quest of establishing self-mastery, goal persistence and positive reappraisal. This area all cognitive and behavioral strategies that can contribute to your emotional well-being. The process of engaging in cognitive restructuring through the recommended guide will allow for substantial changes in your mental landscape.

This is an effective strategy that allows you to focus on and eliminate negative or unreasonable thinking, promoting a realistic and positive mindset. You will be able to achieve mastery over anxiety by proactively noticing and modifying these negative thought patterns, creating an atmosphere of improved well-being. Cognitive restructuring is more than just changing one's thoughts; it is a path of self-discovery and empowerment. By challenging and reshaping your mental framework, you establish the groundwork for long-term beneficial transformation. Each modified idea is an achievement toward becoming a more resilient, optimistic, and fulfilled version of yourself.

Therefore, grasp cognitive restructuring's refining power to establish avenues to improved cognitive focus and personal fulfillment Nur et al (2019). It takes a conscious decision to start the transformational path by releasing yourself from the limitations imposed by social norms. The S.O.L.V.E technique helps break through generational norms constraints and cultivate inner confidence on your own. Inner confidence is where personal empowerment begins. This route is significant because it's a deliberate step towards emancipating yourself from other people's expectations and allowing your confidence to grow freely. This procedure provides you with specific guidance for individuals navigating the complex terrain of confidence intertwined with family and customary family expectations. Cultivating self-assurance and empowerment is the goal, and the ground-breaking S.O.L.V.E method is an inspiring invitation to break free from social conventions.

Chapter 9

Chapter 9: Developing Emotional Resilience

Cultivating the Art of Emotional Resilience

Fundamentally, disrupting patterns is not an indication of a complete redesign; rather, it entails a meticulous, purposeful change. You can think of this to be the equivalent of changing obsolete software that has been operating for far too long. Breaking negative patterns takes deliberate effort, a dedication to self-discovery and a determination to "fight against all odds".

This entails comprehending that the fact something has always been done a certain way, is not meant to indicate it's the only or best way for you. Before you engage on this journey, realize that it is an embodiment of progress. This is about releasing yourself from what no longer serves you. You have the opportunity to embrace the exciting freedom that comes with selecting a new path and living a life. This will help you transform into the amazing, uniquely designed soul that you were designed to be.

There are specific, strategic strategies that influence a person's reaction to adversity which is part of building resilience. You can cultivate your resilience by keeping things in perspective, cultivating a positive outlook, and giving self-care first priority American Psychological Association (2011). You may consider resilience to be the ability to bounce back from misfortune and handle pressure well, serving as inspiration for substantial growth in people. This will help you adopt deliberate habits and cultivate a resilient attitude that can weather life's storms. You will be stronger, with the skills necessary to turn setbacks into chances for personal development. Developing resilience is a process that shapes you into a more capable and adaptive version of yourself, not just a matter of getting back up after a setback. We move further to in-depth recommendations for positive solutions. I'll begin by acknowledging certain limiting ideas that have been passed down through generations. Self-doubt, fear of failure, or a lack of confidence are examples of these. *Are you ready to shed the ineffectual labels that previous generations imposed on you?* It's time to disconnect yourself from the world of restricting beliefs passed down like a negative inheritance.

Start to pull up your sleeves and get down to business, beginning with identifying the chains that have kept you back for considerably far too long. Think of insecurity as a silent assassin that lurks in the shadows of your mind, casting shadows on your capacity for achievement. *How frequently have you doubted your abilities, value, or capability to achieve your goals beyond the stars?* If you start to take into account this destructive companion it is the first brave step towards escape. Fear of failing is an ongoing killjoy that has overwhelmed countless hopes. It's like an immortal haunting your ambition's avenues, expressing tales of an impending demise. You have the chance now to turn on the lights and tackle this fear.

Recognize it, acknowledge it, and then show it the exit door because you aspire to pursue, and failure is simply another obstacle on the way to achievement. The absence of conviction is an unattainable substance that seems to be just out of reach. *Do you ever doubt whether you're sufficiently talented, clever enough, or capable enough?* It's a common issue, and acknowledging it is not an expression of shortcomings, but rather an indicator pointing toward places suitable for development. Let us now discuss the origins of these restrictive beliefs, which are frequently rooted in biological influences. It's not about pointing fingers or allocating blame; it's about accepting that our parents, despite their love and good intentions, have shortcomings as human beings with problems. Self-doubt, fear of failure, and lack of confidence may have been subconsciously passed down like an unpleasant ancestral legacy.

Breaking free means recognizing these inherent limitations without condemnation. You are intentionally cutting away the layers, figuring out where these ideas originate from, and deciding whether they belong on the journey. It's a process of exercising your power, realizing that you have the authority to revise your life's narrative and redefine your self-perception. Remember that knowing the past is more important than dwelling on it as you go on this journey of awareness. If you have an understanding of those limiting ideas, give them your signature of approval and then declare boldly that you are prepared to share your story. Breaking away from these limiting assumptions is the first step toward finding constructive solutions.

This calls for consciously challenging and questioning the reality of inherited phobias, recognizing them as obstacles that can be conquered. It's past time to break free from the bonds of hereditary beliefs that have held you captive for far too long.You are on a transforming journey in which the first step is stomped with a strong affirmation that you're ready to question, challenge, and overcome these barriers. Let's speak about limiting assumptions ...those subtle whispering in your head that have convinced you of what you can't accomplish, what you're not capable of, or where you should be treading carefully. It's like carrying a suitcase packed with stones around, every hypothesis weighing you down. Recognizing them is not a sign of weakness; instead, it is a battle cry, a tenacious declaration that you are ready to shed the excess weight. It's past time to break free from the bonds of hereditary beliefs that have held you captive for far too long. You have started to embark on a transforming journey in which the first step is taken with a strong affirmation that you're ready to question, challenge, and overcome these barriers.

Let's speak about limiting assumptions ..those subtle hints in your head that have convinced you of what you can't accomplish, what you're not capable of, or where you should be negotiating cautiously. It's like carrying a large backpack containing stones around with you, every expectation weighing you down. Recognizing them is not a sign of weakness; instead, it is a battle cry, a tenacious declaration that you are ready to shed the excess weight. Throughout this process, you may start to question the truth of hereditary problems not to dismiss them as unimportant; rather, it is to acknowledge that they are manageable. Fears may thrive in the shadows of the unidentified by nature. They lose their power when you shine a light on them when you confront them with inquiry and courage.

They are no longer invisible hurdles, but rather steps in the right direction. I want you to envision the fact that you can stand tall among the shattered preconceptions you have faced during your trajectory while having a smile on your face. Identifying these phobias as conquerable barriers is like opening a fascinating new era in your life; one in which you become the hero, the main character who tackles challenges head-on and triumphs. As you take the very first step towards identifying constructive answers, keep in mind that it is more than simply a step; it is a declaration of your willingness to challenge the established status. The path ahead is highlighted by the brilliance of your determination, and what lies before you is a future unencumbered by the weight of limiting assumptions. You are now more equipped to overcome difficulties and embrace limitless opportunities. This is where you recognize their intrinsic transforming power. This means embracing the ability to change, personal growth, and the development of a story that is consistent with one's genuine self.

Prepare for a revolution in your story because you are about to enter the captivating domain of acknowledging your groundbreaking aptitude. It's time to eliminate your previous epidermis, accept change, and start on a personal growth path that is not only disruptive but also authentic to the essence of who you are. We will now explore recognition; the act of comprehending and genuinely perceiving the life-altering potential that you possess. It's like discovering a hidden treasure under the soil of habit and inherited perspectives. In the process of discovering this hidden treasure, you will recognize that change is not the adversary, but rather the driving force for your evolution.

The decision you made to accept your potential to change is not a sign of weakness; it is proof of your strength. It's about being like a coconut tree that bends but does not break in a storm. It's the recognition that, like a river cutting its way through the mountains, you can determine the course of your life. As you stand at the crossroads of recognition, transformation, and personal progress, remember that this is not a race; it is a persisting path of self-discovery. The redefining potential within you is not a distant vision; it is a reality simply patiently waiting to be discovered. You just have to be ready to accept change and encourage personal development. We will now analyze the metrics for personal empowerment. Taking charge of the journey. Let's look at ways to change your thinking and develop more positive solutions to help you achieve your goals. You can now transition to the point of shifting from the perspective of generational limits and start to recognize your capacity for immense transformation. You will start to comprehend and develop the art of redirecting your thinking, creating positive alternatives, and accepting the unconventional transition from generational constraints to your boundless power for change.

The first step in this process is to advance your thought habits. Revisit your thoughts, think of them as an abandoned path…a trail of thoughts that once served a purpose but now feels like an area of depression. It will take time to shift your thinking; recognizing that these well-worn roads may be redirected and rerouted toward optimism and prosperity. Think of positive thinking as a hidden strength. It is like a torch shedding light on the dark narrow paths of difficulties. It is not about ignoring difficulties, but rather about finding productive solutions to them. Changing your perspective involves tackling problems with a mindset that sees possibilities in every stumbling block and solutions in every setback. Now comes the turning point from the viewpoint of generational constraints.

Envision your break-free moment from emotional captivity passed down through the generations. The moment that you are able to acknowledge your capacity for substantial adjustment is a fundamental shift that reshapes the landscape of your possibilities. Generational boundaries are like invisible shutters that have kept you restricted. However, *guess what?* You are not a prisoner; you are an unrestrained individual in a position to rise above the clouds. The incredible regeneration power within you is the key to opening doors that you never knew existed. I want you to think about this critically on a more personal level. Consider a specific aim or dream that you've been nurturing. Changing your mindset involves navigating from *"Can I?" to "How can I?"* You are subsequently replacing self-doubt with self-inquiry and discovering that your potential can be influenced by the options you're prepared to explore in the present, not by limitations of the past. Remember that altering your thinking is not about erasing your past, but rather about redirecting your perspective. Positive answers have been waiting for you to uncover them, and your incredible capacity for transformation is the GPS device guiding you into unknown territories of personal improvement.

Positive solutions motivate you to take control of your story. This requires revising your life script, focusing on your strengths, aspirations, and unlimited opportunities for achievement. You venture through a process of learning how to cultivate courage and overcome restrictive ideas. Effective solutions inspire confidence to confront inherited concerns, cultivating bravery in the face of substantial change. You have the power to redefine your path and create a legacy that truly matters. Positive solutions are more than simply methods; they're the keys to opening the doors to your incredible potential.

You are learning to aggregate the skill of taking charge, changing your life script, and gaining the confidence required to set yourself free from confining assumptions. Positive solutions are more than simply band-aids; they are powerful accelerators that propel you forward. They are the guiding principles that reveal the door to your dreams, strengths, and the plethora of possibilities waiting for you to seize. Think of these as your superhuman strength, allowing you to take control of your story's trajectory and transform the ordinary into the extraordinary. Consider yourself the guide and curator of your unique adventure. You hold the chalk to redraw the scenes, redefine the characters, and design an ending that reflects your goals. Positive solutions necessitate a shift from focusing on limitations to showcasing your strengths, and from focusing on hurdles to focusing on unlimited potential for achievement. Reflect on your life experience as a vibrant, constantly modified lesson plan that has outlined the steps to grasp each lesson. achievement. Reflect on your life experience as a vibrant, constantly modified lesson plan that has outlined the steps to grasp each lesson.

Whenever faced with a challenge, what decisions would you make as the main character? How could you use these strengths to overcome challenges? Your life story is a perpetual syllabus that awaits your modifications. These changes should be in line with the powerful, courageous version of yourself that you are striving to become. You can now start to critically examine the principles of developing bravery and overcoming restrictive beliefs as key tools in your educational toolkit for personal progress using the S.O.L.V.E method. You may notice a gradual shift from panic to proactive problem-solving, a sign of your building emotional resilience.

Behavioural modifications serve as guideposts along your transforming path, pointing you in the direction of authenticity and freedom. These transitions are not isolated events, but rather seeds planted in your garden of personal development. Each day you have the opportunity to discover budding plants, each adding to the developing story of your release. As you break free, you may notice behavioural changes in numerous facets of your life. It could be your communication style, the chances you're willing to take, or the boundaries you set. Think of those times when you surprised yourself by responding differently than expected. This self-awareness serves as a compass, directing you towards more focused and powerful living. Emotional resilience is a series of actions including inner strength, adaptation, and self-compassion. Imagine yourself as the lead performer, effortlessly handling life's problems with a newfound sense of balance. The choreographic process of emotional resilience is about navigating through obstacles with grace rather than avoiding them. Examine how your emotional reactions change in the face of adversity. If a setback used to fill you with despair, notice if you now have a reservoir of strength within, the ability to see setbacks as opportunities for growth.

Emotional resilience enables you to embrace the dance, whirling through challenges without losing your primary focus. The development of positive behaviour and emotional resilience will produce ripples that impact on every coast of your well-being. Reflect on this ripple effect to be the framework that assists in modifying the structure of your life... mental, emotional, and social. As you progress, examine the influence of your changing behaviours on your mental health. *Do you feel empowered, as if you have control over your choices?* Take note of how enhanced emotional resilience transcends emotional well-being and permeates your relationships.

Genuine connections bloom when you reply to other m a place of strength rather than emotional distress. Reflective techniques can help you interpret behaviours and create emotional resilience. These practices function as mirrors, helping you to see the intricacies of your inner world. They offer a safe space for self-awareness, which is essential to your transformational journey. Journaling is a form of reflection that is extremely helpful. Start to document instances of behavioural alterations and emotional responses regularly. This technique not only increases self-awareness but also serves as a documentation of your progress, a tangible witness to your liberation path. *What caused these changes? How did you get around them?* Regular Confirmation, which is frequent assessment, enables the identification of potential problem areas. It allows you to modify techniques based on what works best for you in breaking free from problems. Frequent assessment may also serve as a form of reflective thinking depending on the method chosen. Taking the time to assess progress promotes self-awareness and a better knowledge of how transformation works.

Validating personal advancement is an acknowledgment of one's development. It helps to cement the idea that your trajectory is about evolving into a more empowered version of yourself. As outlined in the S.O.L.V.E method, regular evaluation allows you to constantly alter your tactics. It is the realization that breaking free is a dynamic process that requires adaptability. Consider fine-tuning your techniques based on what works best for you, similar to modifying a ship's sails to manage changing winds. Consider the methods you've used to overcome genetic difficulties. *Have you discovered a deeply satisfying relaxation practice? Or a goal-setting technique that motivates you?*

Regular evaluation forces you to tweak and improve these strategies, making them more personalized and effective. Frequent evaluation may be considered to be a type of reflective thinking; imagine reflective thinking as turning on the light in a previously dark room. It's about getting perspective on your journey, comprehending the different aspects of your actions, and decoding the technicalities of your emotional response. Take a reflective moment in which you consider a recent decision or behavioural change. Analyze why you made that decision and how it relates to your break-free path. Reflective thinking is not about judgment but understanding; return to these observations in the late afternoon, acknowledging successes and identifying growth opportunities. This discipline not only strengthens self-awareness but also grounds your efforts to break free in intentional life. The language you use in self-evaluation is important. Adopt a vocabulary of growth that defines challenges as opportunities and setbacks as learning opportunities.

You may view this vocabulary adjustment as altering the narrative of your emancipation journey. It's all about redefining difficulties as steppingstones and building a mindset that thrives on constant change. Instead of saying, "*I failed at this*," you could say, "*I've learned something valuable from this experience.*" This minuscule shift in vocabulary offers you the ability to face setbacks with exploration and resilience. It transforms setbacks into growth motivations, integrating your inner dialogue with the hope of emancipation.

Celebrating progress is a profound accomplishment that resonates throughout your entire body. You develop a sense of accomplishment and an inflow of positive emotions, including pride, excitement, and a deep sense of fulfillment. It has an emotional impact that acts as a motivator, encouraging you towards success. Take into account a moment of progress recognition in which you reflect on an important behavioural adjustment. Feel the sense of accomplishment flourish in your chest, the warmth of excitement streaming through your veins. This emotional impact is not temporary; it remains engraved in your mind, providing an element of enthusiasm during a difficult period. The following are three examples of how SMART goals can be analyzed whether for daily, weekly or to target a specific problem within a specific timeframe. SMART goals are essential for your transformative reflection exercises.

Chapter 10

Chapter 10: A Declaration for Authentic Living

Congratulations.... Though it is the last chapter in your transformational journey; this is not the last action you must take. As you start to discover your true self, you might need to peel back some layers and uncover the real essence that may have been hidden due to expectations from external influences. It can be a scary process, but it's a necessary step to move forward. Remember, your parents love you and want what's best for you, but sometimes their demands can unintentionally limit your individualism. It's all about finding a balance between honoring your familial relationships and cultivating your true self.

It entails making deliberate decisions that align with your own goals and desires. *Are you ready to "grab the bull by the horns? You* have the potential to break the bonds that have restricted your potential. You have a profound S.O.L.V.E toolkit to shape your tactic into breaking free from the fears that have restricted your gifts attest to your entire potential development and unleash your unique gifts. You may discover that this is just not important for individual development. It is advisable to develop an understanding and appreciation of the perspectives of rooted beliefs. If previous patterns were based on adhering to cultural standards, seeking connections with similar ideals becomes revolutionary. It's about finding a circle of fellow human beings who understand your break-free path and share your vision for living with purpose. When you acknowledge the power of making informed choices before responding this serves as a pause button that allows you to consider the impact of your words. This is a significant improvement as opposed to reacting impulsively, this intentional pause encourages thoughtful replies, which aids in the process of breaking free from communication barriers.

You are now evolving further on the trajectory that gently nudges you to assess previous communication practices impacted by generational norms. *Were the reactions pre-programmed and prompted by inherited scripts?* This is where your proactive decision-making modifies these patterns. It's about choosing words that reflect your true personality and directing conversations away from predetermined responses and toward genuine communication. If you can utilize the strategy of establishing deliberate decision-making, this will also foster genuine relationships with people. You may regard this as a process of bridging the gap, where each intentional word deepens the connections of comprehension.

You are then able to create a space for meaningful discourse by pausing and pondering on your comments. This will help you build relationships that transcend generational boundaries. Additionally, this takes into account how relationships improve when deliberate communication takes predominance. Your conversations increasingly become more significant when they are authentic rather than using conventional templates. Your network will start to notice and take into consideration your improved communication approach.

This will create a ripple effect that encourages openness and real expression. You will actualize the benefits of the ripple effect as you prioritize authentic relationships and incorporate deliberate communication into your life. The ripple effect generates a wave of change that transforms not only individual connections but also the collective discussion within your scope of influence. Your emancipation path extends its impact, inspiring others to challenge deeply entrenched communication standards and embrace authenticity. Contemplate how your actions will affect your close connections, network, community as well as future generations. Your dedication to authentic connections serves as an example of emerging away from communication patterns that impose restrictions.

Pledge your dedication to true relationships, embracing honesty, mutual understanding, and shared ideals. As you reflect on this journey, visualize creating your revolutionary communication philosophy. Commit to incorporating thoughtful decision-making into all interactions, transforming conversations into a form of expression that symbolizes your enlightenment path. Your philosophy functions as an affirmation of your commitment to meaningful connections and true self-expression. It reflects the revolutionary attitude of breaking free from inherited communication standards, resolving the way for a life full of true interactions and meaningful interaction.

Let us look at some practical ways to include purposeful communication in your regular interactions. Consider these to be tools in your breaking-free toolkit, each designed to support your progress towards authentic connection-conscious Pause...take a conscious pause before responding in a conversation. This brief pause allows you to examine the impact of your remarks. *"Is this response true to my authentic self?"* you should ask yourself. *"Does it help to create a genuine connection?* "One of the fundamental principles of personal development is to motivate people to act decisively rather than to stand by and let issues happen. The fact that you can actively face and resolve challenging circumstances increases your self-efficacy, develops strong problem-solving abilities, and deeply empowers you. Your proactive approach in addition to transforming obstacles into chances for development, fosters an attitude that values accountability and initiative.

When you take decisive actions, you not only overcome obstacles but also gain the ability to better control your destiny and bring about positive life changes. The ability to assume responsibility spurs your personal development and moves you closer to a stronger, more independent life. Developing positive relationships is important for making connections and accepting help and support from others. Building and nurturing positive relationships can contribute to personal development by providing a support system, fostering a sense of belonging, and promoting emotional well-being American Psychological Association (2011)

Reflective Questions

1. Which specific limiting beliefs and worries are now impeding your personal growth and how can you proactively question and overcome them?

2. How can habitual family routines contribute to feelings of stuckness and what intentional choices can you make to break free from these patterns and embrace positive changes?

3. How can you apply the S.O.L.V.E method to overcome the obstacles generated by limiting beliefs, worries, and family rituals, paving the way for increased self-awareness and fulfillment

4. How will you actively apply the ' S.O.L.V.E approach' in your life to create a new and authentic tale that is true to yourself?

5. What concrete measures can you take this week to retell your story and free yourself from parental judgments and generational expectations?

6. How do you recognize and handle specific instances of self-doubt that may impede your progress and well-being?

7. How does the reoccurring family-related instability affect your mental and emotional health and what strategies may be used to effectively handle these challenges

8. What concrete efforts can you take this week to break free from the cycle of self-doubt and family conflict and create a more positive and empowering mindset?

9. How can you find an appropriate balance between meeting parental expectations and honestly expressing your unique gift?

10. How has the fear of parental expectations influenced the process of uncovering and communicating your unique gift?

11. How will you use the S.O.L.V.E method to unfold your unique gifts and empower yourself to unfold a gift that reflects your true aspirations?

12. What specific moral convictions do you find difficult to defend and by what method could you develop the confidence to do so in challenging situations?

13. In what situations do you feel the most fear of speaking up for your moral views and what strategies can you implement to overcome this fear and act with conviction?

14. How can you use the S.O.L.V.E method to navigate difficult situations, giving yourself the courage and strength to preserve your moral principles

15. What specific life difficulties do you find the most difficult to negotiate while adhering to generational norms and how can you do so without compromising your authentic self?

16. How can you find a balance between honoring tradition and embracing personal growth? What do you think influences your decision-making in the face of life problems?

17. In what manner will you use the S.O.L.V.E technique to confront problems in a way that is consistent with your beliefs and goals, breaking free from restricting generational conventions to build resilience and growth?

18. How do communication hurdles and generational patterns influence your interactions with others, and can you pinpoint specific occasions where these limits are most noticeable?

19. What techniques can you use to break down communication barriers and break free from generational patterns, allowing you to have more authentic and open interactions with others around you?

20.In what ways can you actively practice mindful communication to improve your capacity to truly express yourself and navigate generational communication challenges?

21. What specific limiting beliefs do you recognize in yourself, and how can you devise a strategy to overcome them to pave the way for personal growth?

22.How can you ensure that your personal goals fit with the authentic goals that you see you while to your overall well-being when you set and accomplish them?

23.How will you implement the S.O.L.V.E strategy into your problem-solving approach, converting problems into opportunities for success and personal growth?

24.How do inherited worry patterns appear in your life, and can you indicate particular instances where these patterns are influenced by generational cycles?

25.In what ways can generational cycles contribute to the positive reinforcement of inherited worry habits, and what conscious efforts can you take to change this cycle and alleviate concerns?

26.How can you use the S.O.L.V.E method to break free from the impacts of generational cycles and establish a mindset focused on positive solutions and personal growth?

27. Can you identify specific negative features of your attitude that prevent you from feeling thankful, and how can you intentionally change your perspective to develop a more optimistic mindset?

28. What intentional actions can you take to improve your perspective and acknowledge the good things in life?

29.How are you going to use the S.O.L.V.E technique to get over the obstacles of a negative mindset and constrained perspectives, and cultivate gratitude?

30.Which particular financial limiting beliefs do you hold, and how do these beliefs impact your feeling of economic incapacity?

31. What effects have these restricting beliefs had on your general well-being and financial decisions, and what actions can you take to dispel and combat these ideas?

32.How can you use the S.O.L.V.E technique to empower yourself to make sound financial choices and cultivate a growth-oriented mentality to resolve financial disempowerment resulting from limiting beliefs?

33.In what areas do you believe you lack emotional awareness, and how do you think generational patterns have affected your emotional intelligence?

34.Can you identify generational trends that have shaped your emotional reactions, and to what extent can you intentionally strive to become more emotionally intelligent in certain circumstances?

35.To develop personal growth and resilience in emotional understanding, how will you apply the S.O.L.V.E method to tackle the lack of emotional intelligence associated with generational trends?

36.Can you give examples of particular circumstances in which your inflexible worldview has influenced your ability to make decisions? How might embracing a more flexible viewpoint aid in personal development?

37. How can one use the S.O.L.V.E technique to overcome an established perspective, promote deliberate decisions that support one's personal development objectives, and cultivate an optimistic outlook that leads to positive change?

38.How can you intentionally disconnect yourself from parental projections to cultivate a more compassionate self-view?

39.What effects do parental projections have on your capacity to practice self-compassion?

40. Could you give concrete examples of how your self-perception has been impacted by parental projections? If so, what actions can you take to develop a stronger sense of self-compassion that is unimpeded by external factors?

41. In what way are you going to apply the S.O.L.V.E. approach to address the lack of self-compassion resulting from projections from your parents, giving yourself the capacity to overcome established routines and cultivate a self-love and understanding mindset?

42.Where do cultural expectations affect your self-confidence, and in which particular circumstances do those standards make it challenging for you to assert yourself?

43. Can you identify instances where cultural expectations have affected your self-confidence?

44. How can you leverage the S.O.L.V.E method to help overcome culturally imposed doubts and establish a mentality that enables you to embrace your authenticity and face obstacles with greater assurance?

45.What particular limiting assumptions do you have about your career, and how have expectations from your family influenced these assumptions?

46.Can you identify deliberate decisions that comply with personal principles to overcome expectations from family members?

47.In what way can you use the S.O.L.V.E technique to break through career-related limiting beliefs so that you can make intentional choices that support your genuine goals and advance your career?

48.Which aspects of your life do you believe are inconsistent in line with your personal goals along with how you conduct yourself, and what triggers this imbalance?

49.Are you able to identify situations in which outside factors have caused you to deviate from your own values?

50.How may the S.O.L.V.E process help you reconcile the discrepancy between your actions and your goals to ensure that you can lead a more purposeful and consistent life?

51. Can you identify any relationship in which you find it difficult to set boundaries, and how do family expectations affect your ability to do so in these particular situations?

52.Can you spot trends where your ability to set healthy boundaries has been hampered by familial expectations, and what deliberate decisions can you make to adjust these boundaries?

53. How can you use the S.O.L.V.E method to help you deal with the difficulty of establishing boundaries in relationships that are defined by family expectations so that you can help others feel empowered and independent?

54.What specific expectations prevent your quest for personal fulfillment, and how have society's expectations triggered your separation from your passions?

55.In what ways do you believe societal conventions limit your desires, and can you name particular instances where these expectations have impacted your quest for fulfillment?

56.Which actions can you take to break away from society's expectations and reconnect with your passions, allowing you to live a truer and fulfilled life?

57. How do your present behaviours connect with your overall wellness goals, and are any impeding your progress?

58.Are you able to track any behaviours that have had a negative or positive impact on your physical and mental health?

59.Can you identify any harmful habits that may be limiting your path to total wellness?

60.Are you able to identify limiting beliefs preventing the next generation of leaders from developing to their full potential, and how may these beliefs be recognized and overcome?

61. Could you give particular instances of how your own limiting beliefs have affected the way you have raised emerging leaders? What deliberate decisions can you make to support a growth-oriented mindset?

62.In the context of leadership development, how might the S.O.L.V.E method be used strategically for overcoming limiting beliefs, enabling you to help influence the next generation of leaders who are more self-assured and empowered?

63.Which particular societal expectations do you find most restrictive, and how can you establish a balance between them and your desire for privacy by being aware of these demands?

64.When it comes to setting boundaries that respect your personal space as well as your social obligations, can you think of any situations in which you felt at odds with society's expectations? If so, what conscious choices did you make?

65. How can you incorporate the S.O.L.V.E technique to help you effectively set and communicate boundaries when navigating the difficult task of establishing balance between social demands and the need for personal space?

66.What specific factors lead you to feel disconnected from your spiritual practices and beliefs, and how might a better comprehension of these issues help you to realign yourself with your spiritual path?

67. Thinking back to times when you experienced a sense of detachment, what deliberate efforts can you take to integrate spiritual practices into your everyday life so that your beliefs and conduct are in equilibrium?

68.How can you transform your story and make deliberate decisions to cultivate a more profound connection with your spiritual practices and beliefs while using the S.O.L.V.E method to handle the difficulty of spiritual disconnection?

69.When you think back on instances where you had trouble establishing a balance between your independence and shared experiences, what particular obstacles or beliefs might be at play, and how might you overcome them?

70.What deliberate actions can you take to encourage honest dialogue and mutual understanding guaranteeing a healthy balance in your relationships?

71. Using the S.O.L.V.E method's principles, can you rethink how you would approach personal independence in partnerships, releasing restricting ideas and establishing more powerful and harmonious goals

72. When you reflect on the past, what particular instances or trends have led to trust problems in your close connection, and how can you initiate a conversation to resolve these issues?

73. How can you use the S.O.L.V.E method to take an active role in establishing trust, resolving anxiety from the past, and cultivating a more stable intimate relationship?

74. What deliberate steps can you take when dealing with trust issues to create a climate of open discussion, candidness, and comprehension between both sides?

75. What actions can you take to increase your exposure to a broader spectrum of networks and viewpoints when you contemplate breaking free from restrictive habits and promoting personal growth?

76. How could you actively explore ways to engage with people from various cultures using the S.O.L.V.E method to promote a more inclusive and diverse outlook on life?

77. How can you actively engage with varying communities and embrace different perspectives to push yourself beyond your comfort zone and further your personal development?

78.Given the possible effects on your sense of purpose and personal development, how can you use your resources and abilities to actively participate in social issues and promote community well-being?

79. How can you break free from any limiting ideas that hinder you from getting involved in social causes that you are passionate about?

80.How can you commit to social causes as part of everyday activities that you participate in, such that your actions support community well-being and further your personal development?

Reference Page

American Psychological Association (2011). "Building Your Resilience Retrieved from https://www.apa.org/topics/resilience-building

Johannes et al (2019). Mindfulness and leadership: Communication as a behavioral correlate of leader mindfulness and its effect on follower satisfaction Retrieved from https://psycnet.apa.org/

Nur Hani Zainal and Michelle G. Newman (2019). "Relation Between Cognitive and Behavioral Strategies and Future Change in Common Mental Health Problems Across 18 Years" American Psychological Association Pages 1, 2 , 4, 7 , 8, 18

Palmer Chris (2020) "Harnessing The Power of Habits" Monitor on Psychology, American Psychological Association (APA)., Vol. 51, No 8

Allison A Johnson is a Professional Teacher/ Trainer, Author and Educator from Jamaica W.I.

She may be contacted via email at alijay.johnsongmail.com

Connect with her on social media using the link below for LinkedIn: